TRUE STORIES IN THE NEWS

by Sandra Heyer

A BEGINNING READER

Longman

Introduction

TRUE STORIES IN THE NEWS is a high-beginning reader for students of English as a Second Language. It consists of 22 units centered around human-interest stories adapted from newspapers and magazines. The vocabulary and structures used in the stories are carefully controlled to match those of a typical beginning ESL course. At the same time all attempts were made to keep the language natural.

PRE-READING.

A photograph introduces each unit. Pre-reading questions based on these photographs are suggested to motivate the students to read, to encourage predictions about the content of the reading, and to aid in understanding difficult vocabulary.

READING THE STORY.

A three-step process is suggested for reading the story. After the pre-reading activities the students read the story silently two times, once without stopping, then stopping to circle new vocabulary.

When all the students have finished reading, the teacher clarifies the meaning of new vocabulary, perhaps making reference to the vocabulary exercises to encourage guessing vocabulary from context clues.

Finally the teacher reads the story aloud while the students follow along in their texts. Teachers, should, of course adapt whatever reading strategies best suit their classes.

THE EXERCISES.

Each unit offers a variety of post-reading exercises. Both the choice and the use of the exercises are flexible and will depend on the individual teaching environment and style. The exercises might be used for pair or small-group work, or for programmed instruction, with the teacher selecting exercises to match the needs of particular students. The exercises can also be used in a teacher-centered classroom. The vocabulary and comprehension exercises can be completed orally or in writing. The perforated answer key at the back of the book affords the teacher a choice in the method of correcting the exercises. Students can work independently, in pairs, or in small groups, verifying their answers against those in the answer key. Or the instructor can lead the students in answering the questions. The exercises could also be assigned as homework.

Vocabulary. The vocabulary exercises are designed to aid comprehension by helping define unfamiliar words. Some of the exercises encourage guessing meaning through context clues; others introduce paraphrasing; still others ask students to guess meaning by answering ''or'' questions based on the text. All the exercises try to discourage students from relying on bilingual dictionaries and to rely instead on pictures, titles, context clues, and other sources to discover meaning.

Comprehension. The comprehension exercises are not intended to test the students' understanding of the reading as much as to introduce reading skills which will foster comprehension while helping to clarify meaning.

Understanding the Main Idea is a multiple choice exercise. It asks the students to choose an appropriate title for the reading and to look at the main ideas.

Understanding Details recycles some of the vocabulary from the vocabulary exercises, verifies comprehension, and encourages the development of scanning techniques. The latter can be further exploited by having students scan for self-correction.

Understanding Pronouns are exercises in identifying pronoun referents. Pronouns relate sentences of a text to each other and enrich the texture of a written passage by eliminating the need to repeat nouns. The pronoun exercises are seen not as grammar exercises, but as a tool to aid comprehension and illustrate paragraph cohesion.

Finding Information asks the students to skim for answers to specific questions about the reading.

Understanding Cause and Effect focuses the students' attention on causal relationships expressed by words such as *because* and *so*.

Making Inferences helps the student interpret underlying meaning in the text. These exercises ask the student to judge the validity of statements based on their understanding of the reading, and to support their opinion with references to statements in the text.

Reviewing the Story offers an opportunity for students to retell the story. A modified Cloze passage, this exercise recycles vocabulary, encourages recall of information, simplifies and abbreviates the story so that students can see the text in a new form, and practices scanning, asking the students to self-check by looking back at the story.

Discussion and Writing. Two spin-off exercises end each unit. A discussion section asks students to personalize the ideas and themes presented in each reading by discussing questions with classmates, completing ranking exercises, filling in graphs, solving problems, and talking about language. It is hoped that these discussions will provide further pleasure from the reading process and give insights into cultural similarities and differences.

The final exercise is a guided writing based on the reading.

The exercises are not included to be a struggle for the students. The reading selections and exercises in *TRUE STORIES IN THE NEWS* are intended to offer pleasure in reading by building the students' confidence along with their reading skills, and by stimulating their imagination and interest in things incredible but true.

Contents

1. PRE-READING

Look at the picture.

- Where are these people?
- What are they doing?
- What is a ferris wheel?

Love on the Ferris Wheel

THE people in the picture are at an amusement park. They are riding on the ferris wheel. Their names are Jim and Ann.

Do you know what Jim and Ann are doing? They are getting married! A minister is riding on the ferris wheel, too. You can't see him in the picture. He is sitting in the seat in front of Jim and Ann. The minister is marrying Jim and Ann.

Jim and Ann are getting married on the ferris wheel. That is unusual. Something else is unusual. Jim is the man on the left of the picture. He is wearing a white dress. He is holding flowers. Ann is the woman on the right. She is wearing a black suit and a tie. Why is Jim wearing a dress? Why is Ann wearing a suit and a tie?

Ann told Jim, ''I want to marry you. But I don't like cooking and cleaning and taking care of a house. I want to be a businesswoman. I don't want to be a wife.''

''That's OK,'' Jim said. ''I'll be the wife. You can be the husband.'' That is why Jim is wearing a dress and Ann is wearing a suit.

But why are they getting married on the ferris wheel? I don't know!

2. VOCABULARY

Look at the picture and answer the questions.

1. Are the people in the photograph at an *amusement park* or at *home?*
2. Are the people on a *ferris wheel* or on a *sofa?*
3. The minister isn't in the picture, but he is on the ferris wheel, too. He is *marrying* Ann and Jim. Are Ann and Jim a student and a teacher now? Or are they husband and wife?
4. Is the woman in the picture *buying* a suit or *wearing* a suit?

3. COMPREHENSION

UNDERSTANDING THE MAIN IDEA

Circle the letter of the best answer.

1. ''Love on the Ferris Wheel'' is about
    a. the rides at an amusement park.
    b. two people who are getting married on a ferris wheel.
    c. a businessman and a businesswoman.
2. Jim is wearing a dress because
    a. he likes dresses.
    b. he wants to be a woman.
    c. he is saying, ''I'll take care of the house.''

UNDERSTANDING DETAILS

Read the sentences. One word in each sentence is not correct. Find the word and cross it out. Write the correct word.

1. The people in the picture are at an ~~airport~~. *amusement park*
2. A doctor is riding on the ferris wheel, too.
3. Jim is wearing a white shirt.
4. Jim is holding vegetables.
5. Ann is wearing a black skirt and a tie.
6. Ann told Jim, ''I don't want to be a businesswoman.''

UNDERSTANDING PRONOUNS

Look at the pronouns. What do they mean? Write the letter of your answer on the line.

1. _b_ Jim and Ann are riding on *it*.   **a.** the minister
2. ____ *He* is marrying Jim and Ann.   **b.** the ferris wheel
3. ____ Jim is wearing *it*.   **c.** a white dress
4. ____ Ann is wearing *it*.   **d.** taking care of a house
5. ____ Jim is holding *them*.   **e.** flowers
6. ____ Ann doesn't like *it*.   **f.** a black suit

4. DISCUSSION

Think about these questions. Discuss your answers with your classmates.

1. In the United States, a bride usually wears a white dress. A groom usually wears a suit. What does a bride wear in your country? What does a groom wear?
2. In the United States, wedding guests throw rice at the bride and groom. This is a wedding custom. Talk about a wedding custom in your country.
3. You will find wedding rings, flowers, champagne, cake, and rice at most weddings in the United States. Do you find these things at weddings in your country, too?

5. WRITING

Ann didn't want to be a wife. She doesn't like cooking and cleaning and taking care of the house. What about you? Who does these things at your house?

- Who vacuums?
- Who dusts the furniture?
- Who cleans the bathroom?
- Who washes the dishes?
- Who buys the food?
- Who sets the table?
- Who cooks dinner?
- Who makes the bed?
- Who does the laundry?
- Who lies on the sofa and watches TV?

Talk about your answers with a classmate.

You can write a paragraph from the questions and answers. Here is an example.

> At my house my husband and I do the housework. I vacuum, dust the furniture, clean the bathroom and make the bed. I buy the food and cook dinner too. My husband sets the table and washes the dishes. We do the laundry together. Then we both lie on the sofa and watch TV!

Now write your paragraph.

UNIT 2

1. PRE-READING

Look at the picture.

- What is the man eating?
- What is the man putting on his salad?

Dish Soap for Dinner

JOE came home from work and opened his mailbox. In his mailbox he found a yellow bottle of soap—soap for washing dishes.

The dish soap was a free sample from a soap company. The company mailed small bottles of soap to thousands of people. It was a new soap with a little lemon juice in it. The company wanted people to try it.

Joe looked at his free bottle of soap. There was a picture of two lemons on the label. Over the lemons were the words "with Real Lemon Juice."

Joe was happy. "I'm going to eat a salad for dinner," he thought. "This lemon juice will taste good on my salad." He put the soap on his salad and ate it.

Soon Joe felt sick. He wasn't the only person who got sick. A lot of people thought the soap was lemon juice. They put the soap on fish, on salads, and in tea. Later they felt sick, too. Some people had stomachaches. Some people went to the hospital. Luckily no one died from eating the soap.

What can we learn from Joe's story? Read labels carefully. And don't eat dish soap for dinner!

2. VOCABULARY

Complete the sentences. Find the right words. Circle the letter of your answer.

1. The dish soap was a _____ from a soap company.
   a. letter
   b. free sample
   c. mailbox

2. The company wanted people to _____ the soap.
   a. try
   b. eat
   c. mail

3. There was a picture of two lemons on the _____.
   a. soap company
   b. label
   c. salad

4. What can we learn from Joe's story? Read labels _____.
   a. fast
   b. happily
   c. carefully

3. COMPREHENSION

UNDERSTANDING THE MAIN IDEA

Circle the letter of the best answer.

1. "Dish Soap for Dinner" is about
   a. reading labels carefully.
   b. many people in the hospital.
   c. free samples from soap companies.
2. Another good title for this story is
   a. "A Day at the Hospital."
   b. "Soap and Salad."
   c. "Joe's Mailbox."

FINDING INFORMATION

Read the questions. Find the answers in the story. Write the answers.

1. Did Joe find a letter or a free sample in his mailbox?

   Joe found a free sample in his mailbox.

2. Was the free sample from a soap company or from a food company?

   _____

3. Did the soap have tomato juice or lemon juice in it?

   _____

4. Did Joe put the soap on his dishes or on his salad?

   _____

5. Did some people have stomachaches or headaches?

   _____

6. Did some people go to the supermarket or to the hospital?

   _____

UNDERSTANDING DETAILS

Read the sentences. One word in each sentence is not correct. Find the word and cross it out. Write the correct word.

1. In his mailbox Joe found a yellow bottle of ~~beer~~. *soap*
2. The dish soap was a free ticket from a soap company.
3. It was a new soap with a little apple juice in it.
4. The company wanted people to eat it.

5. There was a picture of two bananas on the label.

6. Joe put the soap on his dishes.

7. Soon Joe felt fine.

8. Some people had backaches.

9. Some people went to the library.

4. DISCUSSION

**Labels often have important warnings. The warnings say, "Be careful!"
Look at these pictures and read the warnings. Draw a line and connect the
warning with its meaning.**

1. May cause drowsiness.

2. May be harmful or fatal if swallowed.

3. Flammable.

a. This is poison. Do not eat or drink this. You can die.

b. Do not smoke or use matches here. This can burn easily.

c. You can feel sleepy.

**Look for bottles and cans with warnings on the label. Copy the warnings.
Bring the warnings to class and discuss them.**

5. WRITING

**Read this story. It is in the present tense. Write the story again in the past
tense.**

Joe comes home from work and opens his mailbox. In his mailbox he
finds a free sample of dish soap. The dish soap has a little lemon juice in it.
    Joe looks at his bottle of soap. There is a picture of two lemons on the
label. Over the lemons are the words "with Real Lemon Juice."
    Joe thinks the soap is lemon juice. He puts it on his salad and eats it.
Soon he feels sick. Poor Joe!

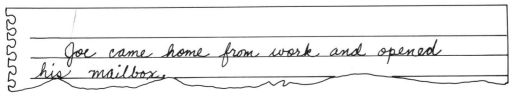

Joe came home from work and opened his mailbox.

---

1. PRE-READING

Look at the picture.

- Why don't these people have any hair?

Fifty Good Friends

MANUEL Garcia had stomach cancer. The doctors told him, ''You need chemotherapy to stop the cancer.''

Manuel went to the hospital for chemotherapy. Chemotherapy is strong medicine. After a few weeks of chemotherapy, Manuel's hair began to fall out. Soon he had no hair.

Manuel was depressed. He looked strange without hair. He didn't want people to see him.

Manuel's brother and three other relatives visited Manuel in the hospital. Manuel was surprised when he saw them. They had no hair! ''You shaved your heads!'' Manuel said. Manuel began to laugh. The other men laughed, too. ''Please be quiet,'' the nurse said. But the nurse was smiling.

Manuel came home from the hospital. Friends and relatives came to visit him. ''We want to shave our heads,'' they said. ''We want to look like you.'' Manuel shaved their heads. He also shaved his sons' heads. In one day he shaved 50 heads. Manuel's wife wanted to shave her head, too. ''No!'' said Manuel.

At the hospital Manuel was depressed because he had no hair. Now he is not depressed. ''I'm ready for anything,'' he says.

2. VOCABULARY

Look at the picture and complete the sentences. Find the right words.
Circle the letter of your answer.

1. The men in the picture are Manuel Garcia's friends and _____.
   a. sisters
   b. teachers
   c. relatives

2. They have no hair because Manuel _____ their heads.
   a. shaved
   b. painted
   c. studied

3. Now they all _____ like Manuel.
   a. walk
   b. talk
   c. look

4. Manuel's friends shaved their heads. Manuel laughed. Now he is not _____. Now he is ready for anything.
   a. happy
   b. depressed
   c. hungry

3. COMPREHENSION

UNDERSTANDING CAUSE AND EFFECT

Find the best way to complete each sentence. Write the letter of your answer on the line.

1. _d_ Manuel Garcia went to the hospital

2. _b_ Manuel's hair fell out

3. _c_ Manuel was depressed

4. _a_ Manuel's friends and relatives wanted to shave their heads

a. because they wanted to look like Manuel.

b. because chemotherapy is strong medicine.

c. because he had no hair.

d. because he needed chemotherapy.

MAKING INFERENCES

Read the sentences below. Some of the sentences are true, and some of the sentences are false (not true). If a sentence is true, circle T. If a sentence is false, circle F. Which sentence from the story helped you? Copy the sentence.

1. Manuel Garcia was very sick.   (T)   F   _Manuel Garcia had stomach cancer._

2. Manuel Garcia is a father.   T   F   _____

_____

3. Manuel has a lot of friends and relatives.   T   F   _____

_____

4. Manuel's wife loves him very much.   T   F   _____

_____

REVIEWING THE STORY

Do you remember the story? Complete each sentence. Then read the story again. Were you right?

Manuel Garcia went to the hospital for chemotherapy. Chemotherapy is strong _medicine_ . Manuel's hair began to fall out. Soon
Manuel had no __hair__ .

Manuel was _____ because he had no hair. Manuel's

brother and three other relatives visited him in the hospital. They had no hair. "You _____ 4 your heads!" Manuel said. Manuel's friends and relatives wanted to look like him. In one day Manuel shaved 50

_____ 5 .

Now Manuel is not depressed. Now he's ready for _____ 6

4. DISCUSSION

Manuel Garcia had a lot of good friends. What about you? Think about a good friend. Talk about your friend with a classmate. Ask each other questions. For example:

- What is your friend's name?
- How old is your friend?
- Where does your friend live?
- Why do you like your friend?
- What do you and your friend like to do together?
- Do you remember a special time you had with your friend?

5. WRITING

Read this story. It is in the present tense. Write the story again in the past tense.

Manuel Garcia has stomach cancer. The doctors tell him he needs chemotherapy.

Manuel goes to the hospital for chemotherapy. After a few weeks of chemotherapy, Manuel's hair falls out. Manuel is depressed. He looks strange without hair.

Manuel's brother and three other relatives shave their heads. Friends and relatives visit Manuel. Manuel shaves their heads. He shaves his sons' heads, too. Soon everybody looks like Manuel—well, almost everybody. His wife wants to shave her head, too. "No!" says Manuel.

Manuel Garcia had stomach cancer.

UNIT **4**

1. PRE-READING

Look at the pictures.

- Who are these people?
- Is the young girl beautiful?
- Is the young woman beautiful?

Before and After

THE girl in the picture on the left is nine years old. She is very shy. At school she doesn't like to stand in front of the class. She wears thick glasses, and she is not very pretty.

The woman in the picture on the right is about 30 years old. She is an actress. Millions of people see her on TV. She is beautiful.

The girl is Morgan Fairchild at age nine. The woman is Morgan Fairchild at age 30. The girl and the woman are the same person.

Morgan Fairchild says, ''When I was a child, I was very shy. I had white hair, white skin, white eyelashes, white eyebrows, and big, thick glasses. Boys never walked me home after school. At school dances, boys never asked me to dance.''

Then Morgan got contact lenses. She began to use makeup. She let her hair grow. She changed into a beautiful woman.

Today Morgan Fairchild is a popular actress. She is also an author. In her book *Super Looks* she gives information about makeup, skin, hair, diet, and exercise. Morgan Fairchild wants to share her beauty ideas wih other women. She says, ''Maybe a shy little girl will read my book. Maybe I can help her. Maybe she, too, can change her life.''

2. VOCABULARY

Think about the story and answer the questions.

1. Do *shy* people like to stand in front of the class or sit quietly in class?
2. Morgan Fairchild wore *thick* glasses. Were her eyes very bad or very good?
3. Does Morgan Fairchild want to *share* her beauty ideas or *learn* some beauty ideas?
4. Morgan Fairchild is an *author*. Did she write a book or a song?

3. COMPREHENSION

UNDERSTANDING CAUSE AND EFFECT

Find the best way to complete each sentence. Write the letter of your answer on the line.

1. _c_ Morgan Fairchild didn't like to stand in front of the class

    a. because she is an actress.

2. ___ She wore thick glasses

    b. because she wasn't pretty.

3. ___ Boys never asked Morgan to dance

    c. because she was shy.

4. ___ Millions of people see Morgan Fairchild on TV

    d. because she couldn't see very well.

UNDERSTANDING PRONOUNS

Look at the pronouns. What do they mean? Write the letter of your answer on the line.

1. _b_ Morgan Fairchild wore *them* when she was nine years old.

    a. makeup

2. ___ *They* never walked Morgan home from school or asked her to dance.

    b. thick glasses

3. ___ Morgan began to use *it*.

    c. Morgan Fairchild's hair

4. ___ *It* is long and blond.

    d. boys

REVIEWING THE STORY

Do you remember the story? Complete each sentence. Then read the story again. Were you right?

The girl on the left wears thick glasses, and she's not very

_pretty_____1_____. The woman on the right is an actress. Millions of

people see her on _____2_____. The girl and the woman are the same

_____3_____. Morgan Fairchild got contact lenses, began to use

makeup, and let her hair grow. She changed into a _____4_____

woman. Morgan Fairchild is also an author now. She writes about

_____5_____.

4. DISCUSSION

In her book, Morgan Fairchild writes, ''This book is about beauty. We all know that beauty is only skin deep. It's what is inside a person that's important.''

How do you choose your friends? How will you—or how did you—choose your husband or wife? What is important to you?

Read the sentences below to a classmate. Your classmate will answer ''That's important'' or ''That's not important.'' Put a check (✓) under the answers. Then answer the questions yourself. Talk about your answers.

CHOOSING A HUSBAND OR WIFE		
He (or she) is	**That's important.**	**That's not important.**
a. handsome (or beautiful).	———	———
b. rich.	———	———
c. honest.	———	———
d. intelligent.	———	———
e. friendly.	———	———
f. a good cook.	———	———
g. nice.	———	———
h. clean.	———	———
i. hard-working.	———	———
j. educated.	———	———

5. WRITING

Read this story. It is in the present tense. Write the story again in the past tense.

Morgan Fairchild is a shy little girl. She has white hair, white skin, and white eyelashes. She wears thick glasses and she is not very pretty. Boys never walk her home from school or ask her to dance.

Then Morgan gets contact lenses. She begins to use makeup, and she lets her hair grow. She changes into a beautiful woman, becomes a TV star, and writes a book about beauty.

Morgan Fairchild was a shy little girl.

UNIT 5

1. PRE-READING

Look at the picture.

- Who lives in this house?
- What is unusual about this house?

Only Snakes Live Here

MRS. Cora Williams wanted to go shopping. She needed her purse, but she couldn't find it. She looked everywhere. Finally she saw her purse on the living room floor, so she reached down for it. Mrs. Williams screamed. A big snake was crawling near her purse. Mrs. Williams ran out of the house.

The next day Mrs. Williams and her family found five more snakes in their house. The snakes were rattlesnakes. Rattlesnakes are poisonous. The Williams family killed four of the snakes, but one snake escaped.

Later Mrs. Williams and her family heard strange sounds in the house. The sounds came from inside the walls. Were snakes inside the walls? The Williams family was afraid. They packed their suitcases and left the house.

The Williams family left their house. The snakes didn't leave. The snakes are still there.

Why are there snakes in the house? Probably some snakes went under the house and laid eggs. The baby snakes grew up and laid more eggs. Soon there were too many snakes under the house. Some of the snakes went up into the house.

How many snakes are in the house? Nobody knows. Maybe 100. Maybe 200. Maybe 300.

What is the Williams family going to do? They don't know. But they are not going back to their house. The house in Pontotoc, Mississippi is empty now. Nobody lives there—only the snakes.

2. VOCABULARY

Complete the sentences. Find the right words. Circle the letter of your answer.

1. Mrs. Williams saw a snake. She doesn't like snakes. She _____ and ran out of the house.
   a. screamed
   b. laughed
   c. answered

2. A snake was _____ on the floor near her purse.
   a. flying
   b. running
   c. crawling

3. The Williams family found five snakes. They killed four snakes, but one snake _____.
   a. stopped
   b. stayed
   c. escaped

4. Mrs. Williams heard strange noises. The unusual _____ came from inside the walls of the house.
   a. sounds
   b. music
   c. laughter

3. COMPREHENSION

FINDING INFORMATION

Read the questions. Find the answers in the story. Write the answers.

1. Was a snake or a baby crawling near Mrs. Williams' purse?

   A snake was crawling near Mrs. Williams' purse

2. Did the Williams family find five more snakes or five more purses?

   _____

3. Were the snakes poisonous or not poisonous?

   _____

4. Were the snakes making sounds outside the house or inside the walls?

   _____

5. Did the Williams family leave the house, or did the snakes leave the house?

   _____

6. Who lives in the house now, the Williams family or the snakes?

   _____

UNDERSTANDING DETAILS

Read the sentences. One word in each sentence is not correct. Find the word and cross it out. Write the correct word.

1. Mrs. Cora Williams wanted to go ~~swimming~~. *shopping*
2. She needed her car, but she couldn't find it.
3. Finally she saw her purse on the living room wall.
4. A big dog was crawling near her purse.
5. The next day Mrs. Williams and her family found five more snakes in their garden.
6. The Williams family packed their lunches and left the house.

UNDERSTANDING PRONOUNS

Look at the pronouns. What do they mean? Write the letter of your answer on the line.

1. _b_ Mrs. Williams needed *it*.   **a.** eggs

2. ____ *They* are poisonous.   **b.** her purse

3. ____ Mrs. Williams and her family   **c.** their house
   heard *them*.

4. ____ The snakes laid *them* under   **d.** strange sounds
   the house.

5. ____ The Williams family left *it*.   **e.** rattlesnakes

4. DISCUSSION

Think about these questions. Discuss your answers with your classmates.

1. The girl in the picture has a pet snake. Do you like snakes? Do you want a snake for a pet?
2. What kind of snakes are there in your country?
3. Do people in your country eat snakes?

5. WRITING

Write about the Williams family.

1. *They killed four snakes.*

2. _____

3. _____

4. _____

Write about the snakes.

1. _____

2. _____

3. _____

4. _____

UNIT **6**

1. PRE-READING

Look at the picture.

- Who are these people?
- Why are they smiling?

Lost and Found

BOB Shafran was happy. He was at a new school, and the other students were friendly. "Hi, Bob!" they said. But some students said, "Hi, Eddy!" Bob didn't understand. He asked another student, "Why do some students call me Eddy?"

"Oh, that's easy to explain," the student said. "Eddy Galland was a student here last year. Now he goes to a different school. You look like Eddy. Some students think that you're Eddy."

One day Bob met Eddy Galland. The student was right. Bob looked like Eddy. Bob and Eddy had the same color eyes and the same smile. They had the same dark, curly hair. They also had the same birthday. And they both were adopted.

Bob and Eddy found out that they were twin brothers. Soon after the boys were born, the Shafran family adopted Bob, and the Galland family adopted Eddy. Bob's family never told him about Eddy, and Eddy's family never told him about Bob.

Later Bob and Eddy found out that they had another brother. His name was David Kellman. Bob and Eddy met David.

David looked like Bob and Eddy. He had the same color eyes and the same smile. He had the same dark, curly hair. He had the same birthday. And he, too, was adopted.

Why did David look like Bob and Eddy? Why did he have the same birthday? You can probably guess. Bob, Eddy, and David are triplets.

2. VOCABULARY

Complete the sentences. Find the right words. Circle the letter of your answer.

1. Look at the photograph of Bob and Eddy. They have the same dark, _____ hair.
   a. dirty
   (b) curly
   c. blond

2. Soon after Bob was born, the Shafran family _____ him. He had a new mother and father, and a new family.
   a. married
   b. fed
   c. adopted

3. Bob didn't know about Eddy. Eddy didn't know about Bob, either. Later Bob and Eddy _____ that they had another brother.
   a. wrote
   b. screamed
   c. found out

4. David looked like Bob and Eddy. They had the same birthday, and they were all adopted. Bob, Eddy and David are _____.
   a. twins
   b. triplets
   c. sisters

3. COMPREHENSION

UNDERSTANDING THE MAIN IDEA

Circle the letter of the best answer.

1. What was "lost and found"?
   - **a.** students
   - **b.** brothers
   - **c.** parents

2. Bob, Eddy, and David were brothers. They didn't know that. Why?
   - **a.** They didn't have the same last name.
   - **b.** They didn't look alike.
   - **c.** Their parents didn't tell them.

UNDERSTANDING DETAILS

Read the sentences. One word in each sentence is not correct. Find the word and cross it out. Write the correct word.

1. Bob Shafran was at a new school, and the other ~~nurses~~ *students* were friendly.

2. Some students said, "Hi, Bob," but some students said, "Hi, Mary."

3. The student told Bob, "You walk like Eddy."

4. Bob and Eddy had the same dark, curly smile.

5. Bob and Eddy found out that they were twin sisters.

6. Bob, Eddy, and David are twins.

UNDERSTANDING CAUSE AND EFFECT

Find the best way to complete each sentence. Write the letter of your answer on the line.

1. _*d*_ Bob Shafran was happy at his new school

2. ____ Bob never saw Eddy at school

3. ____ Some students called Bob "Eddy"

4. ____ Bob Shafran didn't know he had a brother

   a. because Eddy went to a different school.

   b. because Bob looked like Eddy Galland.

   c. because his family never told him about Eddy.

   d. because the other students were friendly.

4. DISCUSSION

Bob looked like Eddy and David. Who do you look like? Do you look like your sister or brother? Do you look like your mother or your father? Do you have a picture of the person that you look like? Show the picture to the class. Talk about that person.

5. WRITING

Answer the questions. Write your answers in complete sentences.

Ann Gomez
658 Elm Street
Centerville, CA

Hair	Eyes	Height	Weight
Brown	Brown	5-05	120

Date of Birth 9-14-65   L46931

Kathy Gomez
658 Elm Street
Centerville, CA

Hair	Eyes	Height	Weight
Brown	Brown	5-05	118

Date of Birth 3-12-63   L99735

1. Do Ann and Kathy have the same last name?

_____

2. Do Ann and Kathy live at the same address?

_____

3. Do Ann and Kathy have the same color hair?

_____

4. Do Ann and Kathy have the same color eyes?

_____

5. Are Ann and Kathy the same height?

_____

6. Are Ann and Kathy the same weight?

_____

7. And do Ann and Kathy have the same birthday?

_____

You can write a paragraph from the questions and answers. You can begin:

Ann and Kathy are sisters. They live at the same address.

Now write your story.

UNIT 7

1. PRE-READING

Look at the picture.

- Who are these people?
- Why is the man tired?

A Little Traveler

VICENTE Cabrera is a farmer. His farm is near Tecate, Mexico. He works in the fields every day. His son, Tomas, is three years old. Tomas often goes to the fields with his father. Mr. Cabrera works, and Tomas plays.

One day Mr. Cabrera was working in a field. Tomas was sitting on a rock nearby. Mr. Cabrera looked up from his work. Tomas was not on the rock. Mr. Cabrera looked for Tomas. Tomas was not in the field. Mr. Cabrera looked everywhere. He couldn't find Tomas.

The Cabrera farm is close to the United States-Mexican border. There is a fence at the border. But there are holes in the fence. ''Maybe Tomas crawled through a hole in the fence,'' Mr. Cabrera thought. ''Maybe Tomas is in the United States.''

The Mexican police telephoned the U.S. Border Patrol. ''We need your help,'' they said. The Mexican police told the U.S. Border Patrol officers about Tomas. The U.S. Border Patrol officers began to look for Tomas in the United States. They were worried. The land near the border is desert. It is hot in the daytime and cold at night. A small boy can't live long in the desert.

Tomas disappeared on Friday afternoon. On Saturday night a U.S. Border Patrol officer saw small footprints in the sand. He followed the footprints to a bush. Under the bush he found Tomas. Tomas was cold, hungry, and thirsty. He had cuts on his feet and face. But he was alive. He was 15 miles[1] from his home.

[1]24 kilometers

2. VOCABULARY

Complete the sentences. Find the right words. Circle the letter of your answer.

1. The Cabrera farm is close to the United States-Mexican border. A _____ is at the border. It separates the United States from Mexico.
   a. restaurant
   b. museum
   c. fence

2. But there are _____ in the fence, and a small boy can crawl through them.
   a. flowers
   b. rocks
   c. holes

3. Tomas _____ on Friday afternoon. A U.S. Border Patrol Officer found Tomas on Saturday night.
   a. disappeared
   b. worked
   c. changed

4. Tomas walked in the desert for 15 miles. A U.S. Border Patrol Officer found his small _____ in the sand.
   a. coins
   b. footprints
   c. purses

3. COMPREHENSION

FINDING INFORMATION

Read the questions. Find the answers in the story. Write the answers.

1. Is Vicente Cabrera a teacher or a farmer?

   Vicente Cabrera is a farmer.

2. Is his farm in the United States or in Mexico?

   _____

3. Is there a hole in Mr. Cabrera's fields or in the fence?

   _____

4. Did Tomas go to the United States or to Mexico?

   _____

5. Did a U.S. Border Patrol officer find Tomas under a bush or under the sand?

   _____

6. Was Tomas dead or alive?

   _____

7. Was Tomas two miles or 15 miles from his home?

   _____

UNDERSTANDING PRONOUNS

Look at the pronouns. What do they mean? Write the letter of your answer on the line.

1. _c_ Tomas was sitting on *it*.   **a.** footprints

2. ____ Tomas crawled through *it*.   **b.** the desert

3. ____ The Mexican police telephoned *them*.   **c.** a rock

4. ____ *It* is hot in the daytime and cold at night. **d.** a bush

5. ____ A U.S. Border Patrol officer saw *them* in the sand. **e.** the U.S. Border Patrol

6. ____ The officer found Tomas under *it*.   **f.** a hole in the fence

MAKING INFERENCES

Read the sentences below. Some of the sentences are true, and some of
the sentences are false (not true). If a sentence is true, circle T. If a
sentence is false, circle F. Which sentence from the story helped you?
Copy the sentence.

1. Vicente Cabrera works very   (T)   F   *He works in the*
   hard.   *fields every day.*

2. Mr. Cabrera was worried   T   F   _____
   about Tomas.
                                            _____

3. The U.S. Border Patrol   T   F   _____
   cannot help the Mexican
   police.   _____

4. Tomas went far from his   T   F   _____
   home.
                                            _____

4. DISCUSSION

Think about these questions. Discuss your answers with your classmates.

At some time, almost every child is lost for a few minutes. Children often
get lost in a supermarket, a store, or a park. When you were a child, were
you ever lost? How did you feel? Was your child ever lost? How did you
feel?

5. WRITING

Write about Vicente Cabrera.

1. *He is a farmer.* _____

2. _____

3. _____

4. _____

Write about Tomas.

1. _____

2. _____

3. _____

4. _____

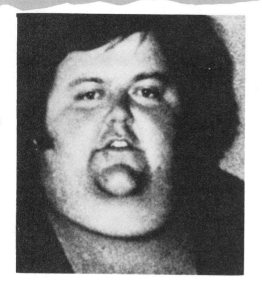

1. PRE-READING

Look at the pictures.

- Who is the man in the first picture?
- Who is the man in the second picture?
- What are the man and woman doing?

A New Man

THE man in the first picture lives in Northern Ireland. His name is Roley McIntyre. Roley McIntyre was big. He was very big. He weighed 600 pounds.[1]

For lunch Roley ate ten pieces of bacon, four eggs, ten potatoes, and fried vegetables. For dinner he ate meat and more potatoes, and after dinner he always ate dessert. Before he went to bed, he ate a few sandwiches and some cake.

Roley couldn't drive a regular car. He was too big. He couldn't fit in the front seat. Roley had a special car. It had no front seat. Roley could drive his car from the back seat.

One day Roley went to the doctor. The doctor said, "Mr. McIntyre, you have a special car. Now you need to buy a special coffin—a coffin for a very big man. You have to lose weight, or you're going to die soon."

Roley went on a diet. For breakfast he ate cereal with nonfat milk. For lunch he ate baked beans on toast. For dinner he ate fish and vegetables.

Roley began to lose weight. He met a pretty woman. Her name was Josephine. Josephine told Roley, "Don't stop your diet."

Roley didn't stop his diet. He continued to lose weight. In 18 months he lost 400 pounds.[2]

On August 17, 1985, Roley and Josephine got married. You can see them in the picture. Roley and Josephine are wearing a pair of Roley's old pants.

[1] 272 kilograms
[2] 181 kilograms

---

2. VOCABULARY

Complete the sentences. Find the right words. Circle the letter of your answer.

1. After dinner Roley always ate _____.
   a. lunch
   b. dessert
   c. breakfast

2. Roley couldn't drive a regular car. He was too big. He couldn't _____ in the front seat.
   a. fit
   b. stand
   c. see

3. The doctor told Roley, "You have a special car. Now you need to buy a special _____ because you're going to die soon."
   a. refrigerator
   b. garage
   c. coffin

4. The doctor told Roley, "You are too big. You have to go on a diet. Don't eat potatoes and dessert. You need to _____."
   a. eat more
   b. lose weight
   c. buy clothes

3. COMPREHENSION

UNDERSTANDING DETAILS

Read the sentences. One word in each sentence is not correct. Find the word and cross it out. Write the correct word.

1. Before Roley went to bed, he ate a few chairs ~~and some~~ *sandwiches* cake.

2. Roley couldn't drive a regular car because he was too small.

3. The doctor said, ''You have to lose money, or you're going to die soon.''

4. Josephine told Roley, ''Don't continue your diet.''

5. In the picture Roley and Josephine are wearing a pair of Roley's old shoes.

UNDERSTANDING CAUSE AND EFFECT

Find the best way to complete each sentence. Write the letter of your answer on the line.

1. _____ Roley McIntyre was big

2. _____ Roley couldn't drive a regular car

3. _____ Roley needed to buy a coffin

4. _____ Roley ate only fish and vegetables for dinner

5. _____ Roley and Josephine could wear a pair of Roley's old pants

a. because he was going to die.

b. because he was on a diet.

c. because he ate a lot.

d. because he couldn't fit in the front seat.

e. because the pants were very big.

REVIEWING THE STORY

Do you remember the story? Complete each sentence. Then read the story again. Were you right?

Roley McIntyre was very big. He _____*weighed*_____ 600 pounds.
                                        1
Roley couldn't drive a regular car. He couldn't fit in the front

_____, so Roley's car had no front seat. He could drive
              2

his car from the _____ seat.
                            3

Roley's doctor said, ''Mr. McIntyre, you have to lose weight, or you're going to _____4_____.'' Roley went on a

_____5_____. He began to lose _____6_____. He met

a pretty _____7_____. She told Roley, ''Don't _____8_____

your diet.''

   Roley didn't stop his diet; he lost 400 _____9_____. And on

August 17, 1985, Roley and Josephine got _____10_____.

4. DISCUSSION

Think about these questions. Discuss your answers with your classmates.

1. Americans worry about their weight. Do people in your country worry about their weight, too?
2. Most American women want to be thin. Many Americans think thin women are beautiful. Do people in your country think thin women are beautiful?
3. What do people eat on a diet? What don't they eat?

5. WRITING

Read the sentences. The sentences are about people who are in this book.

- Roley had to lose weight, so he went on a diet. (Unit 8)
- Manuel's friends wanted to look like Manuel, so they shaved their heads. (Unit 3)
- The Williams family was afraid, so they left their house. (Unit 5)

The sentences below are about people who are not in this book. Complete the sentences. There are many correct ways to complete the sentences.

1. I was cold, so I _closed the window_____.

2. My friend was tired, so she _____.

3. We were thirsty, so we _____.

4. Maria's car was dirty, so she _____.

5. David was hungry, so he _____.

6. Mr. Jones needed stamps, so he _____.

7. Tom's refrigerator was empty, so he _____.

1. PRE-READING

Look at the picture.

- What is the woman holding in her right hand?
- What is the woman holding in her left hand?
- Why is she holding these things?

The Coin

IT was December 25, 1972. Marie Orr, a 13-year-old Australian girl, was happy. It was Christmas, and Marie's mother made a special cake for dessert. She put four small coins into the cake. The four coins were for good luck.

After dinner Marie and her family ate the cake. When they finished the cake, there were three coins on the table. One coin was missing. Marie's mother didn't notice.

After Christmas Marie got sick. She coughed. She couldn't speak. After six weeks she felt better, but she still couldn't speak. Marie went to the hospital.

Doctors at the hospital looked at Marie. They took an x-ray. Marie's parents asked the doctors, "Why can't Marie talk?" The doctors said, "We don't know. Maybe she will speak again. Maybe she won't. We're sorry, but we can't help her."

For 12 years Marie didn't speak. She grew up. She got a job. She got married. But she never spoke.

One day when Marie was 25 years old, she got a sore throat at work. She began to cough. She coughed up a lot of blood. She also coughed up something small and black. What was it? Marie didn't know. She took it to the hospital. A doctor at the hospital said, "This is a coin!"

The doctor told Marie, "I think you can speak again." Marie went to a special doctor and soon she was talking.

What a story Marie can tell!

2. VOCABULARY

Think about the story and answer the questions.

1. Marie's mother put four coins in a special cake for dessert. After dinner there were three coins on the table. Was one coin *added,* or was one coin *missing?*

2. Marie's mother didn't *notice* the missing coin. Did she count the coins on the table, or didn't she count them?

3. Marie got a sore throat at work and began to *cough.* Did she look like picture 1?   Or did she look like picture 2?

4. Marie coughed up a *coin.* Is a dollar bill a coin, or is a penny a coin?

3. COMPREHENSION

UNDERSTANDING THE MAIN IDEA

Circle the letter of the best answer.

1. Marie didn't speak because

   a. a coin was in her throat.

   b. she didn't want to.

   c. a doctor said, "We can't help her."

2. Now Marie can

   a. work again.

   b. bake cakes.

   c. speak again.

UNDERSTANDING DETAILS

Read the sentences. One word in each sentence is not correct. Find the word and cross it out. Write the correct word.

1. It was Christmas, and Marie's mother made a special ~~salad~~ *cake* for dessert.

2. She put four small spoons into the cake.

3. After Christmas Marie got angry.

4. She went to the supermarket.

5. Teachers at the hospital looked at Marie.

6. One day when she was 25 years old, Marie got a sore arm at work.

7. She went to a special doctor and soon she was walking.

UNDERSTANDING PRONOUNS

Look at the pronouns. What do they mean? Draw a line to your answer and circle the word.

After (Marie) ate the Christmas cake, *she* got sick. Six weeks later Marie felt better, but *she* still couldn't speak. Doctors at the hospital said, "*We* can't help Marie."

For 12 years Marie didn't speak. Then one day *she* coughed up something small and black. Marie took *it* to the hospital.

A doctor at the hospital said, "This is a coin!" The doctor told Marie, "*I* think *you* can speak again."

4. DISCUSSION

Marie's mother put coins in the Christmas cake because it is a Christmas custom in Australia. Every country has holiday customs. Talk about a holiday custom from your country.

5. WRITING

Marie was happy because it was Christmas. Marie's mother put coins in the Christmas cake because it is a Christmas custom in Australia.

What is your favorite holiday? Write about the special things people do during your favorite holiday.

1. PRE-READING

Look at the picture.

- What is this picture?
- What happened here?

Buried Alive

IN 1865, in a small town in Germany, a little boy was very sick. His name was Max Hoffman.

"Will our son die?" Max's parents asked the doctor.

"Maybe," the doctor said quietly. "Stay with Max. Keep him warm. That's all you can do."

For three days Max lay in his bed. Then he died. He was only five years old.

Max's parents buried their son in the town cemetery. That night Max's mother had a terrible dream. She dreamed that Max was moving in his coffin. She screamed in her sleep.

"Sh, sh," her husband said. "It's all right. You had a bad dream."

The next night Max's mother screamed in her sleep again. She had the same terrible dream.

On the third night Max's mother had another bad dream. She dreamed that Max was crying. She got out of bed and got dressed. "Quick! Get dressed," she told her husband. "We're going to the cemetery. I want to see Max. I want to dig up his coffin."

At four o'clock in the morning Max's parents and a neighbor hurried to the cemetery. They dug up Max's coffin and opened it. There was Max. He looked dead. But he wasn't lying on his back. He was lying on his side.

Max's father carried Max home. Then he ran to get the doctor. For an hour the doctor rubbed whiskey on Max's lips and warmed his body. Then Max opened his eyes. Max was alive! A week later he was playing with his friends.

Max Hoffman died—really died—in the United States in 1953. He was 93 years old.

2. VOCABULARY

Think about the story and answer the questions.

1. Look at the photograph. Did Max's parents *bury* him in the town cemetery or in the town hospital?
2. Max's mother had a *terrible dream*. Did she laugh and go back to sleep, or did she scream and wake up?
3. Max's mother wanted to see her son, but he was buried in the cemetery. She *dug up* his coffin. Did she put his coffin into the ground, or did she take his coffin out of the ground?
4. "Quick! Get dressed! We're going to the cemetery," Max's mother told her husband. They *hurried* to the cemetery. Did they go slowly or fast?

3. COMPREHENSION

UNDERSTANDING DETAILS

Read the sentences. One word in each sentence is not correct. Find the word and cross it out. Write the correct word.

1. In 1865, in a small ~~lake~~ *town* in Germany, a little boy was very sick.

2. For three days Max lay in his bathtub; then he died.

3. Max's parents buried their son in the town library.

4. That night Max's mother had a wonderful dream.

5. She laughed in her sleep.

6. Max's parents and a neighbor dug up the coffin and closed it.

7. Max's father carried Max home and ran to get the teacher.

8. For an hour the doctor rubbed whiskey on Max's lips and warmed his body; then Max opened his books.

UNDERSTANDING PRONOUNS

Look at the pronouns. What do they mean? Draw a line to your answer and circle the word.

(Max Hoffman) died when *he*₁ was five years old. His parents buried *him*₂ in the town cemetery. That night and the next night Max's mother had a terrible dream. *She*₃ dreamed that Max was moving in his coffin.

On the third night Max's mother dreamed that Max was crying. *She*₄ told her husband, "*I*₅ want to dig up Max's coffin."

Max's parents and a neighbor hurried to the cemetery. *They*₆ dug up Max's coffin and opened *it*₇. Max was lying on his side.

A week later *he*₈ was playing with his friends.

MAKING INFERENCES

Read the sentences below. Some of the sentences are true, and some of the sentences are false (not true). If a sentence is true, circle T. If a sentence is false, circle F. Which sentence from the story helped you? Copy the sentence.

1. 250,000 people lived in Max Hoffman's town.   T (F)   *...in a small town,*
   in Germany,...

2. Max's mother enjoyed her dreams.　T　F　_____

_____

3. When Max's parents buried their son, he was lying on his back in the coffin.　T　F　_____

_____

4. Soon Max got better.　T　F　_____

_____

5. Max lived a long time.　T　F　_____

_____

4. DISCUSSION

Think about these questions. Discuss your answers with your classmates.

1. Is the story "Buried Alive" a true story? Is it possible? Some doctors say it's possible. What do you think?
2. Imagine you are Max Hoffman. You are now an old man. You are talking to a newspaper reporter. Tell the story of "Buried Alive" in your own words.

5. WRITING

Write 6 sentences about yourself. Write 3 true sentences, and 3 sentences that are not true. For example:

■ I want to go to the moon. (true)
■ I was a soldier in my country. (not true)

Read your sentences to a classmate. Can your classmate guess the true sentences? Can your classmate guess the sentences that are not true?

1. PRE-READING

Look at the picture.

- Who is this woman?
- Why does she have that sign?
- What did she do?

The Winning Ticket

THERESE Costabile is a cashier at a big drug store in Cupertino, California. People buy medicine, makeup, shampoo, garden tools, watches, and toys at the drug store. They pay Ms. Costabile. They also pay her for their lottery tickets.

At the drug store people buy tickets for the California State Lottery. They pay one dollar for a lottery ticket. Then they look at the pictures on the ticket. Some pictures are winning pictures. Some pictures are losing pictures. Most people win nothing. Some people win two dollars. A few lucky people win thousands of dollars.

One day Ms. Costabile was working at the drug store. She sold three lottery tickets to a woman. The woman looked at the pictures on the tickets. Then she threw the tickets on the counter and walked away.

Ms. Costabile picked up the woman's tickets. One ticket was a winning ticket for $50,000.

"Excuse me," Ms. Costabile called to the woman. "You won $50,000."

The woman walked back to the counter. "I thought they were all losing tickets," she said. She took the winning ticket and looked at it. "Thanks," she said. Slowly she walked away.

Why did Ms. Costabile give the woman the ticket? Why didn't she keep the ticket? Didn't she want the $50,000?

"Of course I wanted the money," Ms. Costabile said. "But it was her ticket. It wasn't my ticket."

Ms. Costabile telephoned her mother. She told her mother about the ticket.

"Well, I'm sorry that you aren't rich," her mother said. "But I'm happy that you're honest."

---

2. VOCABULARY

Think about the story and answer the questions.

1. Does a *cashier* take money at a store or at a church?
2. Do children play with *toys* or with *tools?*
3. In a store do people pay in the *basement* or at the *counter?*
4. A man buys a lottery ticket. He wins $5,000. Is his ticket a *losing* ticket or a *winning* ticket?

3. COMPREHENSION

UNDERSTANDING DETAILS

Read the sentences. One word in each sentence is not correct. Find the word and cross it out. Write the correct word.

1. Therese Costabile is a ~~manager~~ *cashier* at a big drug store.

2. She sold three parking tickets to a woman.

3. The woman threw the tickets on the floor and walked away.

4. Ms. Costabile picked up the woman's purse.

5. One ticket was a winning ticket for $5.

6. The woman took the winning ticket and slowly ran away.

7. Ms. Costabile told her uncle about the winning ticket.

8. Her mother said, ''Well, I'm sorry that you aren't rich, but I'm happy that you're friendly.''

UNDERSTANDING CAUSE AND EFFECT

Find the best way to complete each sentence. Write the letter of your answer on the line.

1. __c__ People pay Therese Costabile

2. ____ The woman threw the tickets on the counter

3. ____ Ms. Costabile didn't keep the winning ticket

4. ____ Ms. Costabile's mother was happy

a. because it wasn't her ticket.

b. because her daughter is honest.

c. because she is a cashier.

d. because she thought they were losing tickets.

UNDERSTANDING PRONOUNS

Look at the pronouns. What do they mean? Draw a line to your answer and circle the word.

(Therese Costabile) is a cashier at a big drug store. People pay *her* for the things *they* buy. People also pay Ms. Costabile for their lottery tickets.

One day Ms. Costabile was working at the drug store. *She* sold three lottery tickets to a woman. The woman looked at the tickets and threw *them* on the counter.

Ms. Costabile told the woman, "*You* won $50,000."
5

The woman took the winning ticket and looked at *it*. Then *she* slowly
6   7

walked away.

Ms. Costabile telephoned her mother. *She* told *her* about the ticket.
8   9

"Well," her mother said, "*I*'m happy that *you*'re honest."
10   11

4. DISCUSSION

Think about these questions. Discuss your answers with your classmates.

1. Therese Costabile gave the winning ticket to the woman. The woman
   said, "Thank you" and walked away. She didn't give Ms. Costabile any
   money. Was that OK?
2. Is there a lottery in your country? Do you play the lottery in your
   country? Do you play the lottery in the United States? Do you win
   money sometimes? Do you like to play games for money?

5. WRITING

**Congratulations! You won one million dollars in the lottery! How will
you spend the money? Below are some ideas. Number the ideas from one
to five. Write "1" next to the best idea. Write "5" next to the worst idea.
Talk about your list with your classmates.**

_____ give money to poor people

_____ buy a new house and a new car

_____ visit my family

_____ take a trip around the world

_____ stop working

Now make your own list of the things you will buy and do.

1. PRE-READING

Look at the picture.

- Why is this dog wearing sunglasses?
- Where is he going?

The Luxury Hotel

MARION and David Ten Bruin own a luxury hotel. Every room at the hotel has a thick carpet and air conditioning. Some rooms have TVs, and in every room guests hear soft stereo music. The hotel is not expensive. A room with a TV is only $14 a night.

Do you want to stay at this luxury hotel? Probably not. Sometimes the guests at the hotel are not very polite. They put their feet on the furniture. They jump on the beds. At dinner time, when the guests are hungry, they are very noisy. When they eat, they never use knives, forks, or napkins.

Who are these impolite guests? They are dogs. Mr. and Mrs. Ten Bruin own the Scottsdale Pet Hotel in Scottsdale, Arizona. Sometimes people go away on business or on vacation. Then they leave their pets at the pet hotel. They know the Ten Bruins will take good care of their pets.

Dogs at the pet hotel lie on carpets in air-conditioned rooms. Each dog has a private room. All day the dogs listen to soft stereo music. Some dogs lie in small beds or on sofas and watch TV.

The Ten Bruins walk each dog twice a day. They give fat dogs special diet food. They give sick dogs medicine. And they give dirty dogs baths.

The Ten Bruins take care of other pets, too. Sometimes cats and goldfish stay at the hotel.

Look at the dog in the picture. His owners are going on vacation. The dog isn't going with them. But the dog doesn't care. He has a reservation at the Scottsdale Pet Hotel.

---

2. VOCABULARY

Which words have the same meaning as the words in the story? Circle the letter of the correct answer.

1. Marion and David Ten Bruin *own* a luxury hotel.
   a. have
   b. want

2. In every room guests hear *soft* stereo music.
   a. loud
   b. quiet

3. Do you want to stay at this *luxury* hotel?
   a. first-class
   b. inexpensive

4. Sometimes the *guests* at the hotel are not very polite.
   a. visitors
   b. workers

5. The Ten Bruins walk each dog *twice a day*.
   a. ten times every day
   b. two times every day

6. Sometimes dogs and cats *stay* at the hotel.
   a. are guests at
   b. are owners of

3. COMPREHENSION

FINDING INFORMATION

Read the questions. Find the answers in the story. Write the answers.

1. Do the Ten Bruins own a restaurant or a hotel?

The Ten Bruins own a hotel.

2. Is a room with a TV $14 a night or $140 a night?

_____

3. Are the guests noisy or quiet?

_____

4. Are the guests polite or impolite?

_____

5. Are the guests people or pets?

_____

UNDERSTANDING DETAILS

Read the sentences. One word in each sentence is not correct. Find the word and cross it out. Write the correct word.

1. Marion and David Ten Bruin own a luxury ~~apartment.~~ *hotel*

2. Every room at the hotel has a thick sandwich and air conditioning.

3. Some rooms have TVs, and in every room guests hear loud stereo music.

4. Sometimes the workers at the hotel are not very polite.

5. People leave their children at the pet hotel.

6. Each dog has a private telephone.

7. The Ten Bruins give sick dogs chocolate.

8. Sometimes tigers and goldfish stay at the hotel.

UNDERSTANDING PRONOUNS

Look at the pronouns. What do they mean? Draw a line to your answer and circle the word.

Marion and David Ten Bruin own a luxury hotel. (The hotel) is beautiful, but *it* is not expensive.
¹

Sometimes the guests at the hotel are not very polite. *They* put their feet
2
on the furniture and jump on the beds. The guests are dogs.

People leave their pets at the pet hotel when *they* go away on business or
3
on vacation. *They* know the Ten Bruins will take good care of their pets.
4

4. DISCUSSION

Think about these questions. Discuss your answers with your classmates.

1. Which animals are good pets? Look at the list of animals below. Number
   the animals from one to five. Write ''1'' next to the best pet. Write ''5''
   next to the worst pet. Talk about your list with your classmates.

   _____ a goldfish

   _____ a dog

   _____ a snake

   _____ a bird

   _____ a cat

2. Which animals are popular pets in your country? Do you want a pet?
   Do you have a pet now? What kind of animal is your pet? What is your
   pet's name? What do you feed your pet?

5. WRITING

Write about the Ten Bruins.

1. They own the Scottsdale Pet Hotel.

2. _____

3. _____

4. _____

Write about the dogs.

1. _____

2. _____

3. _____

4. _____

1. PRE-READING

Look at the picture.

■ What are these people doing?
■ What is unusual about that?

I Ran for Everybody

JEFF Keith has only one leg. When he was twelve years old, Jeff had cancer. Doctors had to cut off most of Jeff's right leg.

Every day Jeff puts on an artificial leg. The leg is plastic. With the plastic leg Jeff can ski, ride a bicycle, swim, and play soccer. He can also run.

In the photograph Jeff is running with some young men. They have plastic legs, too. They are wearing special T-shirts. The T-shirts say, "Run, Jeff, Run. Jeff Keith's Run Across America."

In the summer of 1984 Jeff Keith began to run across the United States. He started running in Boston, Massachusetts. He stopped running in Los Angeles, California in February 1985. He ran 3,200 miles[1] in seven months. That's about 16 miles[2] each day. Jeff wore out 36 pairs of running shoes and five plastic legs.

Jeff stopped in cities on the way to Los Angeles. In every city people gave Jeff money. The money is not for Jeff. It is for the American Cancer Society. The American Cancer Society will use the money to learn about cancer.

On the way to Los Angeles Jeff talked to people about cancer. He also talked about being disabled. Jeff is disabled, but he can do many things. He finished college and is studying to be a lawyer. Jeff says, "People can do anything they want to do. I want people to know that. I ran not only for disabled people. I ran for everybody."

[1] 5,150 kilometers
[2] 26 kilometers

2. VOCABULARY

Which sentence has the same meaning as the sentence in the story? Circle the letter of the correct answer.

1. Jeff Keith has only one leg. Jeff *is disabled,* but he can do many things.
   a. Jeff has a physical problem.
   b. Jeff has no father or mother.

2. Every day Jeff puts on an *artificial* leg. The leg is plastic.
   a. Jeff's leg is not real.
   b. Jeff's leg is expensive.

3. In the summer of 1984 Jeff Keith began to run across the United States. He *started* running in Boston, Massachusetts. He stopped running in Los Angeles, California in February 1985.
   a. Jeff liked running in Boston, Massachusetts.
   b. Jeff began running in Boston, Massachusetts.

4. Every week Jeff bought a new pair of running shoes. He *wore out* 36 pairs of running shoes.
   a. Jeff wore his shoes until they were not good.
   b. Jeff wore his shoes outside.

3. COMPREHENSION

UNDERSTANDING THE MAIN IDEA

Circle the letter of the best answer.

1. The main idea of ''I Ran for Everybody'' is
   a. some disabled people wear artificial legs.
   b. disabled people can do many things.
   c. some disabled people are lawyers.
2. Jeff Keith wants us to know that
   a. people can do anything they want to do.
   b. it is 3,200 miles from Boston to Los Angeles.
   c. running shoes are expensive.

FINDING INFORMATION

Read the questions. Find the answers in the story. Write the answers.

1. Did Jeff Keith run across the United States or across California?

   Jeff Keith ran across the United States.

2. Did he run 3,200 miles or 320 miles?

   _____

3. Did he wear out 36 pairs of pants or 36 pairs of running shoes?

   _____

4. Did he talk to people about cancer or about running?

   _____

5. Did people give Jeff money or presents?

   _____

6. Is the money for Jeff or for the American Cancer Society?

   _____

7. Did Jeff run for everybody or only for disabled people?

   _____

REVIEWING THE STORY

Do you remember the story? Complete each sentence. Then read the story again. Were you right?

Jeff Keith has an artificial ___*leg*___₁. It is plastic. Jeff can do

many things with this _____ leg. In the summer of 1984
                              2

Jeff Keith began to _____ across the United States. He
                           3

ran 3,200 miles in seven months. He _____ _____
                                            4   5

36 pairs of running shoes and five plastic legs. In every city people gave

Jeff _____. The American Cancer Society will use the
            6

money to learn about _____. Jeff talked to people about
                             7

cancer and about being _____. Jeff says, "People can do
                               8

anything they want to do. I want people to know that. I ran not only for

disabled people. I ran for _____."
                                   9

4. DISCUSSION

Think about these questions. Discuss your answers with your classmates.

1. Jeff Keith likes to ski and play soccer. Which sports do you like?
2. What is the number one sport in your country?
3. Baseball is the number one sport in the United States. Do you like to
   play baseball?

5. WRITING

Jeff Keith says, "People can do anything they want to do." Here is a list of
some things Jeff wanted to do.

- He wanted to ski.
- He wanted to play soccer.
- He wanted to run from Boston to Los Angeles.
- He wanted to finish college.

What do *you* want to do? Do you want to play the guitar? Do you want to
be a police officer? Do you want to be rich?

Make a list of five things you want to be or want to do.

1. _____
2. _____
3. _____
4. _____
5. _____

1. PRE-READING

Look at the picture.

- Who is this woman?
- How old is she?
- Why is she angry?

The Lucky Thief

LOUISE Burt was walking along a San Francisco street. Suddenly a man took her purse and ran. Mrs. Burt was very angry. She had ten dollars, her bus pass, and the keys to her house in her purse. Mrs. Burt ran after the thief.

The thief ran one block, two blocks, three blocks. Mrs. Burt ran one block, two blocks, three blocks. The thief was a young man. He ran fast. Mrs. Burt was not a young woman. She was 73 years old. But she ran fast, too. Mrs. Burt stayed right behind the thief.

Mrs. Burt was wearing two chopsticks in her hair. The chopsticks had sharp ends. Mrs. Burt took the chopsticks out of her hair. "Maybe I can stab the thief with these chopsticks," she thought. "Then he will drop my purse."

The thief ran into an apartment building. Mrs. Burt followed him. "Help! Stop him!" she shouted. "He has my purse!"

Two police officers were walking near the apartment building. They heard Mrs. Burt and ran to help her. One police officer stayed with Mrs. Burt. The other police officer chased the thief.

The police officer found the thief on the roof of the apartment building. The thief was looking in Mrs. Burt's purse. When he saw the police officer, the thief dropped the purse and jumped off the building. The building was two stories high.

A few minutes later the police officer caught the thief. He was hiding under a car. He couldn't run because he had two broken ankles. The police took the thief to jail. The thief will stay in jail for a long time. But the thief was lucky. He was lucky that the police caught him. He was lucky that Mrs. Burt didn't catch him!

2. VOCABULARY

Read the sentences. Guess the meaning of the words. Circle the letter of the right answer.

1. Louise Burt was walking along a San Francisco street. Suddenly a man took her purse and ran. Mrs. Burt ran after the *thief.*

   (a.) a person who takes other people's things; a robber

   b. a person who studies; a student

2. The chopsticks had sharp ends. "Maybe I can *stab* the thief with these chopsticks," she thought. "Then he will drop my purse."

   a. help with something that has a point

   b. hurt with something that has a point

3. The building was *two stories high.*

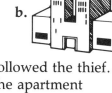

a.   b.

4. The other police officer followed the thief. He *chased* the thief into the apartment building.

   a. put

   b. followed quickly

3. COMPREHENSION

UNDERSTANDING DETAILS

Read the sentences. One word in each sentence is not correct. Find the word and cross it out. Write the correct word.

1. A man took Mrs. Burt's ~~umbrella~~ *purse* and ran.

2. The thief ran slowly.

3. Two police officers were sleeping near the apartment building.

4. One police officer stayed with Mrs. Burt, and the other police officer visited the thief.

5. The thief couldn't run because he had two broken arms.

6. The police took the thief to school.

7. The thief will stay in jail for a short time.

UNDERSTANDING PRONOUNS

Look at the pronouns. What do they mean? Write the letter of your answer on the line.

1. _*d*_ *He* took Mrs. Burt's purse.

2. _____ Mrs. Burt had *them* in her purse.

3. _____ Mrs. Burt was wearing *them* in her hair.

4. _____ *They* ran to help Mrs. Burt.

5. _____ *It* was two stories high.

a. the roof

b. two police officers

c. two chopsticks

d. the thief

e. ten dollars, her bus pass, and the keys to her house

MAKING INFERENCES

Read the sentences below. Some of the sentences are true, and some of the sentences are false (not true). If a sentence is true, circle T. If a sentence is false, circle F. Which sentence from the story helped you? Copy the sentence.

1. Mrs. Burt always carried a lot of money.   T (F)   *She had ten dollars.*

2. The thief was about 45 years old.   T   F   _____

3. The thief will be in jail for   T   F   _____
about two weeks.
_____

4. The thief was happy that he   T   F   _____
took Mrs. Burt's purse.
_____

4. DISCUSSION

Think about these questions. Discuss your answers with your classmates.

1. Picasso was painting when he was 90. Pablo Casals was playing the cello when he was 90. Mrs. Burt chased the thief when she was 73. Do you know an old person who is very active, like Picasso, Pablo Casals, and Mrs. Burt? Talk about that person.
2. About 5% of the old people in the United States live in special homes for old people. About 15% live with their children. Most old people in the United States live in their own houses. Where do most old people in your country live? Where do you want to live when you are old?
3. Are old people important people in the family in your country? How do people show that old people are important? Do Americans think old people are important?
4. What's bad about being old? What's good about being old?

5. WRITING

Write about Mrs. Burt.

1. _She ran fast._ _____
2. _____
3. _____
4. _____

Write about the thief.

1. _____
2. _____
3. _____
4. _____

1. PRE-READING

Look at the picture.

- How old is this woman?
- What does she do?

A Grandmother with Muscles

IN Brooklyn, New York a little girl was playing with some boys. They were riding bicycles and playing ball.

"Diana!" the girl's father called. "Play with the girls! You're a girl, not a boy!"

Diana's father sounded a little angry. But Diana knew that her father was proud of her. He was proud that Diana was strong. He was proud that she was good at sports.

Diana grew up. She stopped playing ball and riding bicycles with the boys. She got married and moved to California. She had two sons. The years went by.

When Diana was 48 years old, she went to a gym. She exercised and lifted weights. She really enjoyed it. At first Diana went to the gym only three days a week. Then she started going every day. She got stronger and stronger. Her muscles got bigger and bigger. Diana became a body-builder. Today Diana Vasquez is a champion body-builder. She has over 24 awards for body-building.

Diana is proud of her awards. But she doesn't exercise and lift weights only to win awards. Diana's father said, "Good health is very important. If you don't have good health, you have nothing." Diana thinks that her father was right. She says, "Body-building keeps me healthy. I feel better today than I did 20 years ago. I can do more things."

Diana says, "Good food is very important for health, too. Diet is 50% of body-building. I don't eat butter or oil. I don't eat a lot of sweets. I eat a lot of fruit, vegetables, yogurt, and rice. I also get plenty of sleep and fresh air."

Body building and eating good food keep Diana healthy and young-looking. Look at the picture of Diana. How old does she look? She is not 25 or 30 years old. She is a grandmother. Diana Vasquez is 51 years old.

2. VOCABULARY

Which sentences have the same meaning as the sentences in the story?
Circle the correct answer.

1. Diana knew that her father was *proud* of her. He was proud that Diana was strong. He was proud that she was good at sports.

   (a.) Diana's father was happy. He thought, "Diana is a wonderful girl."

   b. Diana's father wasn't happy. He thought, "Diana isn't a wonderful girl."

2. Diana is a champion body-builder. She has over 24 *awards* for body-building. Diana is proud of her awards.

   a. Diana got a lot of prizes and money because she is very strong and has very big muscles.

   b. Diana gets a lot of food because she is very strong and has very big muscles.

3. When Diana was 48 years old, she went to a gym. She exercised and *lifted weights*. Her muscles got bigger and bigger.

   a. Diana practiced picking up heavy things and she got stronger.

   b. Diana practiced reading and she got stronger.

4. Diana gets *plenty of* sleep and fresh air.

   a. She gets a lot of sleep and fresh air.

   b. She gets a little sleep and fresh air.

3. COMPREHENSION

UNDERSTANDING DETAILS

Read the sentences. One word in each sentence is not correct. Find the word and cross it out. Write the correct word.

1. Diana's father was proud that Diana was good at ~~sewing.~~ *sports.*

2. When Diana was 48 years old, she went to a museum.

3. She got stronger and stronger, and her feet got bigger and bigger.

4. Today Diana Vasquez is a champion secretary.

5. She has over 24 letters for body-building.

6. Diana's father said, ''If you don't have good food, you have nothing.''

7. Diana says, ''Body-building keeps me hungry.''

UNDERSTANDING PRONOUNS

Look at the pronouns. What do they mean? Write the letter of your answer on the line.

1. _b_ Diana played with *them* when she was a little girl.

2. ____ *He* was proud of Diana.

3. ____ Diana lifts *them*.

4. ____ Diana has over 24 of *them*.

5. ____ Diana thinks *it* is important for good health.

a. her father

b. boys

c. the food she eats

d. awards for body-building

e. weights

MAKING INFERENCES

Read the sentences below. Some of the sentences are true, and some of the sentences are false (not true). If a sentence is true, circle T. If a sentence is false, circle F. Which sentence from the story helped you? Copy the sentence.

1. Diana eats candy, cookies, and cake every day.   T   (F)   "I don't eat a lot of sweets."

2. Diana eats a lot of apples, oranges, and bananas.   T   F   _____

3. Diana sleeps about four   T   F   _____
hours every night.   _____

4. Diana always stays inside.   T   F   _____

_____

5. Diana is often sick.   T   F   _____

_____

4. DISCUSSION

Ask a classmate these questions about diet, exercise, and health. Put a check (✓) under *Yes* or *No*.

	Yes	No
1. Do you eat a lot of fruit and vegetables?	____	____
2. Do you eat a lot of sweets?	____	____
3. Do you take vitamins?	____	____
4. Do you smoke?	____	____
5. Do you drink alcohol?	____	____
6. Do you exercise every day?	____	____
7. Do you get plenty of fresh air?	____	____
8. Do you get plenty of sleep?	____	____

5. WRITING

You can write a paragraph from the discussion questions and answers. Here is an example.

> Anna thinks good health is important. She eats a lot of fruits and vegetables, and she doesn't eat a lot of sweets. She takes vitamins every day. She doesn't smoke. She only drinks alcohol at parties. She exercises every day and she gets plenty of fresh air. She tries to get plenty of sleep, but sometimes she doesn't. Today she is tired.

Now write a paragraph about your classmate.

1. PRE-READING

Look at the picture.

- Where does this boy come from?
- How old is he?
- What is his problem?

This Is the Place for Me

WALTER Polovchak, a 12-year-old boy, was listening to rock 'n' roll music. "Turn off that garbage," his father shouted. Walter turned off the music.

Walter and his family lived in Chicago, Illinois, but they were from the Soviet Union. Walter's father wasn't happy in Chicago. He didn't like American rock 'n' roll. He didn't like his job. He didn't like the weather. He didn't like the food or water. He didn't like Walter's friends or Walter's church. Walter's father and mother decided to go back to the Soviet Union.

Walter didn't want to leave Chicago. He liked his school, and he liked American sports. He liked American food, especially Jello. Walter was happy in the United States. His 18-year-old sister Natalie was happy, too. Walter and Natalie packed their clothes and went to live with a cousin. "We're not going back to the Soviet Union," they said.

Walter's parents said, "Natalie is 18. She can stay in the United States. But Walter is only 12. He has to come with us." Walter's parents called the police. "We want our son," they told the police. The police called the U.S. Immigration and Naturalization Service (INS). The INS said, "Walter can stay in the United States."

Walter's parents went back to the Soviet Union without Walter and Natalie. But first they hired a lawyer. "We want our son," they told the lawyer. "Go to court. Help us get our son back."

The U.S. courts said, "Walter's parents are right. The INS is wrong. Walter has to go back to the Soviet Union." But Walter didn't go back. On October 3, 1985, Walter Polovchak turned 18. He was an adult, so he could live where he wanted. He could live in the United States or he could live in the Soviet Union. He stayed in the United States.

On his birthday Walter got a telegram from his parents. It said, "Best wishes. Congratulations. We wish you well." Walter said, "My parents are happy that I'm here. They know that this is the place for me."

2. VOCABULARY

Which sentences have the same meaning as the sentences from the story?
Circle the letter of the correct answer.

1. Walter was listening to rock 'n' roll music. Walter's father didn't like rock 'n' roll. *"Turn off that garbage,"* he shouted.
   a. Turn off that beautiful music.
   b. Turn off that terrible music.

2. Walter's parents went back to the Soviet Union *without* Walter and Natalie.
   a. Walter's parents went back to the Soviet Union. Walter and Natalie went back to the Soviet Union, too.
   b. Walter's parents went back to the Soviet Union. Walter and Natalie stayed in the United States.

3. "We want our son back," Walter's parents told the lawyer. "Help us *get our son back.*"
   a. Help us. We want our son to live with his cousin.
   b. Help us. We want our son to live with us.

4. On October 3, 1985, Walter *turned* 18.
   a. October 3, 1985 was Walter's 18th birthday.
   b. On October 3, 1985, Walter returned to the Soviet Union.

3. COMPREHENSION

UNDERSTANDING DETAILS

Read the sentences. One word in each sentence is not correct. Find the word and cross it out. Write the correct word.

1. Walter and his family lived in Chicago, Illinois, but they were from the Soviet ~~Onion~~. *Union*

2. Walter's uncle wasn't happy in Chicago.

3. After six days in the United States, Walter's father and mother decided to go back to the Soviet Union.

4. Walter and Natalie washed their clothes and went to live with a cousin.

5. Walter's parents went back to the Soviet Union with Walter and Natalie.

6. Before they left the United States, Walter's parents hired a carpenter.

UNDERSTANDING PRONOUNS

Look at the pronouns. What do they mean? Write the letter of your answer on the line.

1. _e_ Walter's father didn't like *it*.   **a.** a lawyer

2. ____ Walter liked *it*.   **b.** Jello

3. ____ *She* is Walter's sister.   **c.** a telegram

4. ____ Walter's parents hired *him*.   **d.** Natalie

5. ____ Walter's parents sent *it* on his birthday.   **e.** American rock 'n' roll music

UNDERSTANDING CAUSE AND EFFECT

Find the best way to complete each sentence. Write the letter of your answer on the line.

1. _b_ Walter's father and mother weren't happy in Chicago, so   **a.** she can stay in the United States.''

2. ____ Walter and Natalie didn't want to go back to the Soviet Union, so   **b.** they decided to go back to the Soviet Union.

3. ____ Walter's parents said, ''Natalie is 18 years old, so   **c.** he could live where he wanted to live.

4. ____ On October 3, 1985, Walter turned 18, so   **d.** they packed their clothes and went to live with a cousin.

4. DISCUSSION

Walter's father was an immigrant. He had many problems. Here are some of his problems:

- He didn't like his job.
- He didn't like many American things: the food, the water, the music.
- He wanted to go back to the Soviet Union, but his children wanted to stay in the United States.

Look at the picture of this woman. She is an immigrant, too. What are some of her problems? Does she speak English well? Does she have money? Do her children have friends in the United States? Where is her husband? Where will she live?

With a classmate, discuss the woman's problems. Try to give some ways to help her with her problems.

5. WRITING

What don't you like in the United States?

1. _____

2. _____

3. _____

4. _____

What do you like?

1. _____

2. _____

3. _____

4. _____

UNIT 17

1. PRE-READING

Look at the picture.

- Who is this man?
- What does he do?

Thanks a Million

DO you need money? Write a letter to Mr. Percy Ross. Maybe he will give you some money.

Mr. Ross is a rich man, and he likes to give people money. He has a newspaper column. His column is called "Thanks a Million." It is in 200 newspapers. Every week about 7,000 people write letters to Mr. Ross at the newspapers. Mr. Ross reads the letters. Then he sends money to some of the people. Every week Mr. Ross answers three or four letters in his newspaper column.

Who gets money from Mr. Ross? Mr. Ross usually sends money to old people, sick people, and poor children. A mother wrote Mr. Ross, "I have two daughters, ages one and eight. I give the baby one bottle of milk every day. I want to give her two bottles of milk every day, but I don't have enough money. I also want to give my older daughter ice cream sometimes. Can you help me?" Mr. Ross sent the woman a check. "This check will buy much more than milk and ice cream," he wrote.

Sometimes Mr. Ross doesn't send people money. He sends people the things they need— shoes, a smoke alarm, a hearing aid, new pots and pans, or a sewing machine.

Who doesn't get money from Mr. Ross? Mr. Ross usually doesn't send money to young, healthy people. A 16-year-old boy wrote, "I need $900 to buy a good used car. I really need it because I like a girl. She doesn't like me because I don't have a car." Mr. Ross wrote the boy, "You don't need a car. You need a different girlfriend."

Why does Percy Ross give people money? When Mr. Ross was a boy, he was very poor. He worked hard, and now he is a successful businessman. But Mr. Ross remembers when he was poor. He wants to help poor people. And Mr. Ross is getting older. He wants to give all of his money away before he dies. He says, "Who will get my money? I want to decide."

2. VOCABULARY

Which sentences have the same meaning as the sentences from the story?
Circle the letter of the correct answer.

1. Mr. Ross has a newspaper column. His column *is called* "Thanks a Million." It is in 200 newspapers.
   a. Mr. Ross writes for a newspaper every week. The name of his column is "Thanks a Million."
   b. Mr. Ross writes for a newspaper every week. People telephone Mr. Ross at the newspaper.

2. "I want to give the baby two bottles of milk every day, but I don't have *enough* money."
   a. I have a lot of money.
   b. I need more money.

3. Mr. Ross sent the woman a check. "This check will buy *much more than* milk and ice cream."
   a. This money will buy milk and ice cream.
   b. This money will buy milk, ice cream, and many other things.

4. Percy Ross sends money to many people. Mr. Ross wants to *give* all of his money *away*.
   a. Mr. Ross wants to keep his money.
   b. Mr. Ross doesn't want to keep his money.

3. COMPREHENSION

UNDERSTANDING DETAILS

Read the sentences. One word in each sentence is not correct. Find the word and cross it out. Write the correct word.

1. Percy Ross is a ~~poor~~ *rich* man.

2. He likes to give people candy.

3. His column "Thanks a Million" is in 200 states.

4. Every year about 7,000 people write letters to Mr. Ross.

5. Mr. Ross usually sends money to healthy people, old people, and poor children.

6. Mr. Ross worked hard; now he is a successful mechanic.

7. Mr. Ross is getting younger.

8. He wants to give all of his money away before he cries.

UNDERSTANDING PRONOUNS

Look at the pronouns. What do they mean? Write the letter of your answer on the line.

1. _d_ People write *them* to Percy Ross.

2. ____ *They* get money from Mr. Ross.

3. ____ *They* don't get money from Mr. Ross.

4. ____ A boy wanted to buy *one*.

5. ____ A woman wanted to give *it* to her daughter.

a. ice cream

b. a good used car

c. sick people, old people, and poor children

d. letters

e. young, healthy people

MAKING INFERENCES

Read the sentences below. Some of the sentences are true, and some of the sentences are false (not true). If a sentence is true, circle T. If a sentence is false, circle F. Which sentence from the story helped you? Copy the sentence.

1. Percy Ross has about $500 in the bank. T (F) *Mr. Ross is a rich man.*

2. Only a few people read
Percy Ross's newspaper
column.　　　　T　F　_____

_____

3. Many people need money.　　T　F　_____

_____

4. Mr. Ross sends money to
everyone.　　　　T　F　_____

_____

5. When Percy was a boy, he
lived in a big, beautiful
house.　　　　　T　F　_____

_____

4. DISCUSSION

Read these letters. People sent these letters to Percy Ross. Discuss the
letters. What do you think? Which people got money from Mr. Ross?
Which people didn't get money?*

1.
Dear Mr. Ross:
My neighbor is 80 years old.
Yesterday robbers took $200 from
her. Now she has no money. She
cannot buy food. Can you send her
$200?

2.
Dear Mr. Ross:
Please send me $100,000. I need
the money for my family and for
my business.

3.
Dear Mr. Ross:
My mother is 75 years old. She is
in the hospital. The hospital is 25
miles from my home. I want to visit
my mother every day, but I don't
have enough money. I cannot buy
gasoline for my car. Can you send
me money for gasoline?

4.
Dear Mr. Ross:
I want to be an airline pilot, and I
need flying lessons. The lessons
cost $100 an hour. I need 40
lessons. Can you pay for the
lessons?

5.
Dear Mr. Ross:
I am a 24-year-old woman. I'm
going to get married next month.
My problem is this: I can't cook.
Please send me $500 for cooking
school.

*See answer key for Mr. Ross's decisions.

5. WRITING

Write a letter to Percy Ross. Ask him for money for yourself or for
someone you know. Tell him why you need the money.

Dear Mr. Ross:
　　Please send me . . .

1. PRE-READING

Look at the picture.

- What is wrong with the crib?
- What did the babies do?

Don't Eat the Furniture

THE woman in the picture has twin daughters. Their names are Megan and Autumn Beavers. They are 18 months old. Megan is in her mother's arms. Autumn is standing in her crib. Look closely at the crib. Little pieces of the crib are missing. They are missing because Autumn ate them.

When Autumn and Megan were 16 months old, they began to chew on the furniture. At first the twins' mother wasn't worried. All babies chew on things. But the Beavers twins never stopped. And every time they chewed on the furniture, they swallowed the wood. They chewed on the furniture and they ate it, too!

First the twins chewed on their cribs. Their mother moved the cribs out of the twins' bedroom. Then the twins ate the wooden handles on their dresser. Their mother moved the dresser out of the bedroom. There wasn't any wooden furniture in the bedroom, so the twins began to eat the door. In the dining room the twins chewed on the chairs, and in the living room they ate part of a rocking chair.

They ate dirt from the houseplants. They ate more dirt in the garden. Their mother said, ''No!'' again and again, but the twins didn't stop. They kept eating wood and dirt.

Finally the twins went to the doctor. The doctor made several tests. What did the doctor learn? The twins didn't have important minerals. Wood and dirt have these minerals, so the twins ate wood and dirt. The doctor immediately prescribed some medicine. The twins took the medicine and gradually they stopped eating wood and dirt.

The twins don't need to eat wood and dirt any more. They need to take their medicine. And their mother needs to buy some new furniture!

2. VOCABULARY

Which sentence has the same meaning as the sentence from the story?
Circle the letter of the correct answer.

1. They *chewed on* the wood *and* they *swallowed* it.
   a. They coughed up the wood.
   b. They ate the wood.

2. The twins began to eat the wooden *handles* on their dresser.
   a. The twins began to eat picture 1.
   b. The twins began to eat picture 2.

3. They *kept* eating wood and dirt.
   a. They continued to eat wood and dirt.
   b. They liked to eat wood and dirt.

4. The doctor immediately *prescribed* some medicine.
   a. The doctor said, ''Buy this special medicine right now.''
   b. The doctor said, ''See this special doctor right now.''

5. The twins *took* the medicine.
   a. The twins dropped the medicine.
   b. The twins ate the medicine.

3. COMPREHENSION

UNDERSTANDING DETAILS

Read the sentences. One word in each sentence is not correct. Find the word and cross it out. Write the correct word.

1. Autumn and Megan are twin ~~brothers.~~ *sisters*

2. They are 18 years old.

3. When the twins were 16 months old, they began to sit on the furniture.

4. Every time they chewed on the furniture, they swallowed the chairs.

5. First the twins chewed on their arms.

6. Then they ate the handles on their suitcases.

7. They sold dirt from the houseplants.

8. They ate more vegetables in the garden.

UNDERSTANDING PRONOUNS

Look at the pronouns. What do they mean? Write the letter of your answer on the line.

1. _b_ *They* ate wood and dirt.

2. ____ *It* had wooden handles.

3. ____ The twins ate *it* from the houseplants.

4. ____ *She* said ''No!'' again and again.

5. ____ Wood and dirt have *them*.

6. ____ *He* prescribed some medicine.

a. the doctor

b. Autumn and Megan Beavers

c. the dresser

d. minerals

e. the twins' mother

f. dirt

REVIEWING THE STORY

Do you remember the story? Complete each sentence. Then read the story again. Were you right?

When Autumn and Megan were 16 months old, they began to chew on

the ___*furniture*___ . At first their mother wasn't

_____ . All babies like to _____ on
   2   3

things. But the Beavers twins chewed on furniture and _____
the wood. First they chewed on their _____. Then they
chewed on the _____ of their dresser. They ate part of a
rocking _____. They also ate _____
from the garden and from the houseplants.

    Why did they eat dirt and _____? The twins didn't
have some important _____. The doctor prescribed some
_____. Gradually the twins stopped eating _____
and dirt.

4. DISCUSSION

Think about these questions. Discuss your answers with your classmates.

1. The twins ate wood and dirt. Most people do not eat wood and dirt.
   What do people like to eat in your country? Do they eat flowers, insects,
   worms, horses, pigs, dogs, cats, butter?
2. Which American foods do you like to eat? Which American foods don't
   you like to eat?

5. WRITING

Write about the twins.

1. _They chewed on the furniture._
2. _____
3. _____
4. _____

Write about the twins' mother.

1. _____
2. _____
3. _____
4. _____

1. PRE-READING

Look at the picture.

- What is happening?
- Why is the sled on the ice?
- Why are the people in the water?

A Strong Little Boy

CHICAGO, Illinois is next to a big, beautiful lake, Lake Michigan. In the summer Lake Michigan is warm and blue. People lie on the beaches and swim in the water. In the winter Lake Michigan is cold and gray. Snow covers the beaches and ice covers the water.

On a cold January day, a little boy and his father were playing in the snow on a Chicago beach. The boy was Jimmy Tontlewicz. He was four years old.

Jimmy was playing with a sled. He pushed the sled down a small hill. The sled went onto the ice of Lake Michigan. Jimmy ran after the sled. He ran onto the ice. Suddenly the ice broke, and Jimmy fell into the cold water.

Jimmy's father jumped into the water. He couldn't find Jimmy. Minutes went by. He still couldn't find Jimmy. ''My kid is dead! My kid is dead!'' he screamed.

Men from the Chicago Fire Department arrived. Twenty minutes later they found Jimmy and pulled him out of the water. Jimmy was not breathing, and his heart was not beating. He was dead.

At the beach paramedics worked on Jimmy for one hour. He began to breathe and his heart began to beat again. The paramedics rushed Jimmy to the hospital.

Doctors at the hospital put Jimmy in bed on a cold mattress. They wanted Jimmy's body to warm up slowly. They gave him some medicine. They wanted Jimmy to sleep.

After eight days in the hospital Jimmy woke up. He stayed in the hospital for six weeks. Every day he got better. Then he went to another hospital. He stayed there for seven weeks. He began to walk, talk, and play again.

Jimmy was in the water for over 20 minutes. He couldn't breathe in the water. He couldn't get any oxygen. But today he is alive and healthy. How is it possible?

Jimmy is alive because the water was ice cold. Usually the brain needs a lot of oxygen. But when it's very cold, the brain slows down. It does not need much oxygen. So the ice cold water saved Jimmy.

Jimmy's father has another reason. He says, ''Jimmy is alive today because he is a fighter. He is a strong little boy.''

2. VOCABULARY

Which sentences have the same meaning as the sentence in the story?
Circle the letter of the correct answer.

1. Snow *covers* the beaches and ice *covers* the water.
   a. Snow is on the beaches and ice is on the water.
   b. Snow is near the beaches and ice is near the water.

2. The paramedics *rushed* Jimmy to the hospital.
   a. The doctor's assistants took Jimmy to the hospital. They drove fast.
   b. The doctor's assistants took Jimmy to the hospital. They drove slowly.

3. The paramedics *worked on* Jimmy for one hour.
   a. The paramedics helped Jimmy work again. Jimmy worked for one hour.
   b. The paramedics helped Jimmy breathe again. They helped Jimmy for one hour.

4. Jimmy was in the water for *over 20 minutes*.
   a. Jimmy was in the water for more than 20 minutes.
   b. Jimmy was in the water for 20 minutes.

3. COMPREHENSION

FINDING INFORMATION

Read the questions. Find the answers in the story. Write the answers.

1. Was it a cold day in January or a warm day in May?

   It was a cold day in January.

2. Were Jimmy and his father playing in a Chicago park or on a Chicago beach?

   _____

3. Did Jimmy run onto the ice or into the water?

   _____

4. Did Jimmy fall into the warm water or into the cold water?

   _____

5. Who pulled Jimmy out of the water, his father or firefighters?

   _____

6. Was Jimmy in the water for over 2 minutes or for over 20 minutes?

   _____

UNDERSTANDING DETAILS

Read the sentences. One word in each sentence is not correct. Find the word and cross it out. Write the correct word.

1. Chicago, Illinois is next to a big, beautiful ~~mountain.~~ *lake*

2. In the winter Lake Michigan is warm and gray.

3. On a cold January day, a little boy and his father were playing in the sand on a Chicago beach.

4. Suddenly the sled broke, and Jimmy fell into the cold water.

5. Men from the Chicago Fire Department arrived and pulled Jimmy out of the cold snow.

6. The paramedics rushed Jimmy to the church.

7. Today Jimmy is alive and sick.

UNDERSTANDING CAUSE AND EFFECT

Find the best way to complete each sentence. Write the letter of your answer on the line.

1. _d_ Jimmy fell into the cold water

2. ____ Paramedics worked on Jimmy

3. ____ Doctors at the hospital gave Jimmy some medicine

4. ____ Doctors put Jimmy on a cold mattress

5. ____ Jimmy is alive today

a. because they wanted Jimmy to warm up slowly.

b. because they wanted Jimmy to sleep.

c. because the water was ice cold.

d. because the ice broke.

e. because they wanted Jimmy to breathe again.

4. DISCUSSION

Think about these questions. Discuss your answers with your classmates.

Jimmy was under the ice for over 20 minutes. Jimmy's experience was very frightening.

Talk about a frightening experience. When did it happen? What happened? What did you do?

5. WRITING

Read the story. It is in the present tense. Write the story again in the past tense.

Jimmy is playing in the snow on a Chicago beach. His sled goes onto the ice of Lake Michigan. Jimmy chases it. The ice breaks, and Jimmy falls into the cold water.

Twenty minutes later men pull Jimmy out of the water. He is not breathing, and his heart is not beating. Paramedics work on Jimmy for one hour. He begins to breathe and his heart begins to beat. Jimmy is alive. The paramedics rush Jimmy to the hospital.

After 13 weeks in the hospital Jimmy is healthy again. He is a strong little boy.

Jimmy was playing in the snow on a Chicago beach.

1. PRE-READING

Look at the picture.

- Who are these people?
- How many children are there?

A Big Family

IT is early in the morning. Mr. and Mrs. Nason are in the kitchen. They are very busy. Mr. Nason is standing at the stove. He is frying 45 eggs. Mrs. Nason is standing at the kitchen counter. She is pouring 45 glasses of milk. Do Mr. and Mrs. Nason have a restaurant? Are they cooking breakfast for their customers? No, Mr. and Mrs. Nason don't have a restaurant. They are cooking breakfast for their children.

Mr. and Mrs. Nason have 58 children. They adopted 52 of the 58 children. Some of the children are grown. They live in their own houses and have their own families now. But 45 of the children still live at home. Why did Mr. and Mrs. Nason adopt 52 children?

A lot of people want to adopt children. But they want to adopt babies, healthy babies. They do not want to adopt older children or children with physical problems. These children have to wait a long time for a home. Sometimes they never find a home. Mr. and Mrs. Nason want to give some of these children a home and a family.

In the Nason family, everybody helps. Some of the Nason children have physical problems. The children with physical problems help, too. One little girl has no arms, but she changes the baby's diaper. She uses her feet. Mrs. Nason tells the children, "You have a problem. Everybody has a problem. Some people are very short. Some people have glasses. Some people are overweight. Some problems are big, and some problems are small, but everybody has a problem. Don't worry about your problems."

The Nason children help their parents, but Mr. and Mrs. Nason have a lot of work. Mrs. Nason washes 12 loads of laundry every day. Mr. and Mrs. Nason cook all the meals. They are busy from five o'clock in the morning to 11 o'clock at night. How can they do it?

Mrs. Nason says, "God gives everybody different abilities. My husband and I have a special ability. We can love and take care of many children. God said, 'You can do it.' And God is right. We can."

2. VOCABULARY

Think about the story and answer the questions.

1. Mrs. Nason is putting milk into glasses for her 45 children. Is she *pouring* milk, or is she *drinking* milk?
2. Some of the children are *grown*. They live in their own houses and have their own families. Are they the oldest children or the youngest children?
3. Many children don't have a home or a family. Mr. and Mrs. Nason *adopted* 52 of these children. Did they give the children to other people, or did they bring these children into their home?
4. Mr. and Mrs. Nason cook all the *meals*. Do they make breakfast, lunch and dinner, or do they make cookies, cakes, and pies?
5. Mrs. Nason says, "We have a special *ability*. Can Mr. and Mrs. Nason do something special, or can't they?

3. COMPREHENSION

UNDERSTANDING THE MAIN IDEA

Circle the letter of the best answer.

1. "A Big Family" is about
   a. a special family.
   b. a new restaurant.
   c. children with physical problems.

2. Mr. and Mrs. Nason have a special talent. They can
   a. cook all the meals.
   b. love all kinds of children.
   c. be busy all day.

MAKING INFERENCES

Read the sentences below. Some of the sentences are true, and some of the sentences are false (not true). If a sentence is true, circle T. If a sentence is false, circle F. Which sentence from the story helped you? Copy the sentence.

1. The Nasons buy one dozen eggs every week. T (F) *He is frying 45 eggs.*

2. Mr. and Mrs. Nason are about 21 years old. T F _____

3. A lot of people want to adopt 12-year-old boys. T F _____

4. Mrs. Nason uses a lot of laundry soap. T F _____

5. Mr. and Mrs. Nason sleep only six hours every night. T F _____

REVIEWING THE STORY

Do you remember the story? Complete each sentence. Then read the story again. Were you right?

Mr. and Mrs. Nason have 58 ___*children*___ . They
1

_____ 52 of the 58 children. A lot of people want to
2

adopt children. But they want to adopt healthy _____.
_____3_____
They do not want to adopt older children or children with physical

_____. These children have to wait a long time for a
_____4_____

_____. But Mr. and Mrs. Nason want to give them a
_____5_____

_____ and a family.
_____6_____

Mr. and Mrs. Nason have lots of _____. Mrs. Nason
_____7_____

washes 12 loads of _____ every day. She and Mr. Nason
_____8_____

_____ all the meals. They are _____
_____9_____   _____10_____

from five o'clock in the morning to 11 o'clock at night.

Mrs. Nason says, ''My husband and I have a special _____.
_____11_____

We can love and take _____ of many children.''
_____12_____

4. DISCUSSION

Think about these questions. Discuss your answers with your classmates.

1. How many brothers and sisters do you have?
2. How many children do you have? How many children do you want to have?
3. What is good about a big family?
4. What are the problems a big family has?
5. Today most American families are small, with only one, two, or three children. Are families in your country big or small?

5. WRITING

Mrs. Nason says, ''Everyone has abilities.''What are your abilities? Can you cook? Can you fix a car? Can you tell funny stories? Make a list of five things you can do.

1. _____

2. _____

3. _____

4. _____

5. _____

1. PRE-READING

Look at the picture.

- Where are these people from?
- Why are they smiling?

The Bottle

IN December 1979 Dottie and John Peckham, a Los Angeles couple, went to Hawaii on vacation. They traveled by ship.

Some people on the ship threw bottles into the ocean. Each bottle had a piece of paper in it. On each piece of paper were a name, an address, and a message: "If you find this bottle, write to us."

Mrs. Peckham wanted to throw a bottle into the ocean, too. She wrote her name and address on a piece of paper. She put the piece of paper and one dollar into a bottle. She put a cap on the bottle and threw the bottle into the water.

Three years later and 9,000 miles[1] away, Hoa Van Nguyen was on a boat, too. But Mr. Nguyen was not on vacation. He was a refugee from Vietnam. Mr. Nguyen, his brother, and 30 other people were going to Thailand in a small boat. The boat was in the Gulf of Thailand.

There wasn't any drinking water in the boat, and Hoa was thirsty. He saw a bottle in the sea. The bottle was floating near the boat. "What's in the bottle? Maybe I can drink something," he thought. Hoa took the bottle out of the sea and opened it. There wasn't any drinking water in the bottle. But there was a dollar bill. There was also a piece of paper. A name and an address were on the paper. The name was Peckham.

The address was in Los Angeles, California.

Hoa and his brother arrived at the refugee camp in Thailand. Hoa used the dollar; he bought an aerogram and wrote a letter to Mrs. Peckham. "We received a floating mailbox by a bottle on the way from Vietnam to Thailand," Hoa wrote. "Now we send a letter to the boss and we wish you will answer us."

Hoa's English was not perfect, but Mrs. Peckham understood it. She answered Hoa's letter. Hoa wrote another letter, and she answered it, too. For two years Hoa and Mrs. Peckham wrote back and forth. Hoa got married at the camp. The Peckhams congratulated him. Hoa and his wife had a baby boy. The Peckhams sent them money. Finally Hoa asked the Peckhams, "Will you help me and my family? We want to come to the United States."

On April 23, 1985, Hoa Van Nguyen, his wife, their baby, and Hoa's brother arrived at Los Angeles International Airport. Dottie and John Peckham were at the airport. The Nguyens and the Peckhams met at the airport and they all began to cry. Their tears were tears of happiness. "Welcome to the United States of America," Mrs. Peckham said.

[1]15,000 kilometers

2. VOCABULARY

Read the sentences. Guess the meaning of the words. Circle the letter of the right answer.

1. Hoa Van Nguyen was on a boat, too. Mr. Nguyen was not on vacation. He was a refugee from Vietnam. He was going to a *refugee camp* in Thailand.
   a. a place for people without a country (The people cannot live in their own country. They wait here for a home in a new country.)
   b. a place for people on vacation (The people live here in the summer. They play, swim, and enjoy the sun.)

2. Hoa saw a bottle in the sea. The bottle was *floating* near the boat. Hoa took the bottle out of the sea and opened it.
   a. staying on top of the water
   b. staying under the water

3. Mrs. Peckham answered Hoa's letter. Hoa wrote another letter, and she answered it, too. For two years Hoa and Mrs. Peckham wrote *back and forth*.
   a. first in one direction, and then in the other.
   b. four times

3. COMPREHENSION

UNDERSTANDING DETAILS

Read the sentences. One word in each sentence is not correct. Find the word and cross it out. Write the correct word.

1. Dottie and John Peckham traveled to Hawaii by ~~airplane~~ *ship*.

2. Mrs. Peckham threw a bottle into the air.

3. Three days later and 9,000 miles away, Hoa Van Nguyen was on a boat, too.

4. There wasn't any drinking water in the boat, and Hoa was hungry.

5. Hoa took the bottle out of the sea and drank it.

6. Hoa used the bottle; he bought an aerogram.

7. For two years Hoa and Mrs. Peckham telephoned back and forth.

8. Finally Hoa asked the Peckhams, ''Will you visit me and my family?''

9. The Nguyens and the Peckhams met at the airport and they all began to scream.

10. Their tears were tears of sadness.

UNDERSTANDING PRONOUNS

Look at the pronouns. What do they mean? Draw a line to your answer and circle the word.

Dottie Peckham threw a bottle into the ocean. (The bottle) had a piece of paper and a dollar bill in *it*.
1

Three years later Hoa Van Nguyen was on a boat. *He* was a refugee from
2
Vietnam. *He* didn't have any drinking water in the boat. Hoa was thirsty.
3
He saw a bottle in the sea. *He* took the bottle and opened *it*.
4   5   6

Hoa wrote a letter to Mrs. Peckham. His English was not perfect, but
Mrs. Peckham understood *it*. *She* answered Hoa's letter. Hoa wrote
7   8
another letter and Mrs. Peckham answered *it*, too. Finally Hoa asked the
9
Peckhams, ''Will you help me and my family? *We* want to come to the
10
United States.''

On April 23, 1985, the Nguyens and the Peckhams met at the airport and
they all began to cry. ''Welcome to the United States,'' said Mrs. Peckham.
11

MAKING INFERENCES

Read the sentences below. Some of the sentences are true, and some of the sentences are false (not true). If a sentence is true, circle T. If a sentence is false, circle F. Which sentence from the story helped you? Copy the sentence.

1. Hoa Van Nguyen still has the dollar he found in the bottle.

T (F) _Hoa used the dollar._

2. Hoa was not married when he left Vietnam.

T F _____

3. The Nguyen family traveled from Thailand to Los Angeles by ship.

T F _____

4. The Peckhams wanted the Nguyen family to come to the United States.

T F _____

4. DISCUSSION

Think about these questions. Discuss your answers with your classmates.

1. The Nguyens came to the United States on April 23, 1985. When did you come to the United States?
2. The Nguyens came by airplane. How did you come?
3. The Nguyens' trip was 15 hours long. How long was your trip?
4. The Nguyens arrived in Los Angeles. In what city did you arrive?
5. The Nguyens felt tired, but happy. How did you feel?

5. WRITING

Write about Mrs. Peckham.

1. _She is from Los Angeles._
2. _____
3. _____

Write about Hoa Van Nguyen.

1. _____
2. _____
3. _____

1. PRE-READING

Look at the picture.

- Who is this man?
- Why is he smiling?
- What did he do?

Charlie Two Shoes

CUI Zhixi, an 11-year-old boy, hurried along the road from his village in China. He carried a basket of eggs.

U.S. soldiers were at a camp near the boy's village. They were standing around a fire. When they saw the Chinese boy, they said, "Here comes breakfast."

It was November 1945. World War II was over. There was no more fighting. But there wasn't much food in China. Every day the Chinese boy brought some eggs to the U.S. soldiers. The soldiers took the eggs and gave the boy canned food. The soldiers were happy; they had fresh eggs. And the boy was happy; he had canned food.

Day after day the Chinese boy traded food with the soldiers. The Chinese boy liked the soldiers. And the soldiers liked the Chinese boy. But there was a problem. The American soldiers couldn't say the boy's name. They tried and they tried, but they couldn't say "Cui Zhixi." "Cui Zhixi" sounds a little like the English words "two shoes." So, the soldiers called the boy "Charlie Two Shoes."

One day Charlie's father came with Charlie to the soldiers' camp. "Please take my son," he said. "Take good care of him." For the next three years Charlie Two Shoes lived with the American soldiers in their camp. He ate with the soldiers, and he dressed like the soldiers. He wore an American uniform. He went to an American school. The soldiers paid for the school.

In 1948 the soldiers left China. They went back to the United States. They couldn't take Charlie with them. All the soldiers were sad, but one soldier was very sad. His name was Roy Sibit. Roy and Charlie were good friends.

Roy Sibit went back to the United States, but he often thought about Charlie Two Shoes. He was afraid. He thought, "Maybe Charlie is dead." Then, in 1980, Roy got a letter from Charlie. Charlie was alive!

Three years later Charlie came to the United States. He lived with Roy in Ohio. Charlie had a visitor's visa. His visa expired. Charlie couldn't stay in the United States any longer. Roy and Charlie talked to people in the U.S. government and told the people their story. The U.S. government decided to let Charlie stay in the United States. Charlie's wife and three children could come to the United States, too.

Charlie and his family now live in Ohio. They live in a house four miles from Roy Sibit and his family. Charlie is happy because he is near his friend Roy. And Roy is very happy because he is near his friend Charlie.

2. VOCABULARY

Think about the story and answer the questions.

1. Every day the boy brought some eggs to the soldiers and the soldiers gave the boy canned food. Did the soldiers *buy* the eggs with American dollars, or did they *trade* food for the eggs?
2. It was November 1945. World War II was *over*. Was there fighting, or was there no more fighting?
3. Three years later Charlie came to the United States. He had a visitor's visa. Then Charlie's visa *expired*. Could Charlie stay in the United States, or couldn't he stay?
4. The United States government decided to *let* Charlie stay in the United States. Charlie's wife and three children could come, too. Did the government say, "Yes, you can stay," or did the government say, "No, you cannot stay"?

3. COMPREHENSION

UNDERSTANDING DETAILS

Read the sentences. One word in each sentence is not correct. Find the word and cross it out. Write the correct word.

1. Cui Zhixi was a ~~French~~ *Chinese* boy.

2. U.S. dentists were at a camp near the boy's village.

3. World War I was over.

4. Every day the Chinese boy brought some beer to the U.S. soldiers.

5. "Cui Zhixi" sounds a little like the Spanish words "two shoes."

6. For the next three days Charlie Two Shoes lived with the American soldiers in their camp.

7. In 1948 the soldiers went back to England.

8. Charlie came to Ohio on a student visa.

UNDERSTANDING CAUSE AND EFFECT

Find the best way to complete each sentence. Write the letter of your answer on the line.

1. __b__ When the soldiers saw the Chinese boy, they said, "Here comes breakfast"

2. _____ The American soldiers called the boy "Charlie Two Shoes"

3. _____ All the soldiers were sad

4. _____ Charlie lives in Ohio

a. because they couldn't say "Cui Zhixi."

b. because he brought them eggs every day.

c. because he wants to be near his friend Roy.

d. because they couldn't take Charlie with them to the United States.

REVIEWING THE STORY

Do you remember the story? Complete each sentence. Then read the story again. Were you right?

World War II was over. There was no more fighting. But there wasn't much ___*food*___ in China. Day after day the Chinese boy
1
_____ food with the soldiers.
2

The soldiers couldn't say "Cui Zhixi," so they called the boy "Charlie

_____ _____.'' For the next three years

Charlie Two Shoes lived with the American _____ in
                                                    5
their camp.

   Roy Sibit went back to the United States, but he often thought about

Charlie Two Shoes. He was afraid Charlie was _____.
                                                         6
Then Roy got a _____ from Charlie.
                        7
   Charlie came to the United States. He lived with Roy in Ohio. Charlie

had a visitor's _____. Charlie's visitor's visa
                       8
_____. The U.S. government decided to _____
        9   10
Charlie and his family stay in the United States.

4. DISCUSSION

The American soldiers couldn't say ''Cui Zhixi.'' The Chinese words were
difficult for them. Here are some English sentences and phrases. They are
difficult for English-speaking people to say.

- She sells sea shells by the seashore.
- Peter Piper picked a peck of pickled peppers.
- Rubber baby buggy bumpers
- Betty Botter bought some butter.
- Toy boat. Toy boat. Toy boat.

**Say these sentences and phrases fast. Are they difficult for you to say,
too? These sentences are called ''tongue twisters.'' Share a tongue twister
from your country with the class.**

5. WRITING

Write about Charlie.

1. *He lived with the American soldiers.*

2. _____

3. _____

Write about the soldiers.

1. _____

2. _____

3. _____

Answer Key

UNIT 1

Vocabulary
1. The people in the photograph are at an amusement park.
2. The people are on a ferris wheel.   3. They are husband and wife.   4. The woman in the picture is wearing a suit.

Understanding the Main Idea
1. b   2. c

Understanding Details
1. airport/amusement park   2. doctor/minister
3. shirt/dress   4. vegetables/flowers   5. skirt/suit
6. businesswoman/wife

Understanding Pronouns
1. b   2. a   3. c   4. f   5. e   6. d

UNIT 2

Vocabulary
1. b   2. a   3. b   4. c

Understanding the Main Idea
1. a   2. b

Finding Information
1. Joe found a free sample in his mailbox.   2. The free sample was from a soap company.   3. The soap had lemon juice in it.   4. Joe put the soap on his salad.
5. Some people had stomachaches.   6. Some people went to the hospital.

Understanding Details
1. beer/soap   2. ticket/sample   3. apple/lemon
4. eat/try   5. bananas/lemons   6. dishes/salad
7. fine/sick   8. backaches/stomachaches
9. library/hospital

Discussion
1. c   2. a   3. b

Writing
  Joe came home from work and opened his mailbox. In his mailbox he found a free sample of dish soap. The dish soap had a little lemon juice in it.
  Joe looked at his bottle of soap. There was a picture of two lemons on the label. Over the lemons were the words "with Real Lemon Juice".
  Joe thought the soap was lemon juice. He put it on his salad and ate it. Soon he felt sick. Poor Joe!

UNIT 3

Vocabulary
1. c   2. a   3. c   4. b

Understanding Cause and Effect
1. d   2. b   3. c   4. a

Making Inferences
1. T Manuel Garcia had stomach cancer.   2. T He also shaved his sons' heads.   3. T In one day he shaved 50 heads.
4. T Manuel's wife wanted to shave her head, too.

Reviewing the Story
1. medicine   2. hair   3. depressed   4. shaved   5. heads
6. anything

Writing
  Manuel Garcia had stomach cancer. The doctors told him he needed chemotherapy.
  Manuel went to the hospital for chemotherapy. After a few weeks of chemotherapy, Manuel's hair fell out. Manuel was depressed. He looked stange without hair.
  Manuel's brother and three other relatives shaved their heads. Friends and relatives visited Manuel. Manuel shaved their heads, too. He shaved his sons' heads, too. Soon everybody looked like Manuel—well, almost everybody. His wife wanted to shave her head, too. "No!" said Manuel.

UNIT 4

Vocabulary
1. Shy people like to sit quietly in class.   2. Her eyes were very bad.   3. Morgan Fairchild wants to share her beauty ideas.   4. She wrote a book.

Understanding Cause and Effect
1. c   2. d   3. b   4. a

Understanding Pronouns
1. b   2. d   3. a   4. c

Reviewing the Story
1. pretty   2. TV   3. person   4. beautiful   5. beauty

Writing
  Morgan Fairchild was a shy little girl. She had white hair, white skin, and white eyelashes. She wore thick glasses and she was not very pretty. Boys never walked her home from school or asked her to dance.
  Then Morgan got contact lenses. She began to use makeup, and she let her hair grow. She changed into a beautiful woman, became a TV star, and wrote a book about beauty.

UNIT 5

Vocabulary
1. a   2. c   3. c   4. a

Finding Information
1. A snake was crawling near Mrs. Williams' purse.   2. The

Williams family found five more snakes.   **3.** The snakes were poisonous.   **4.** The snakes were making sounds inside the walls.   **5.** The Williams family left the house.   **6.** The snakes live in the house now.

Understanding Details
1. swimming/shopping   **2.** car/purse   **3.** wall/floor
4. dog/snake   **5.** garden/house   **6.** lunches/suitcases

Understanding Pronouns
1. b   **2.** e   **3.** d   **4.** a   **5.** c

UNIT 6

Vocabulary
1. b   **2.** c   **3.** c   **4.** b

Understanding the Main Idea
1. b   **2.** c

Understanding Details
1. nurses/students   **2.** Mary/Eddy   **3.** walk/look
4. smile/hair   **5.** sisters/brothers   **6.** twins/triplets

Understanding Cause and Effect
1. d   **2.** a   **3.** b   **4.** c

UNIT 7

Vocabulary
1. c   **2.** c   **3.** a   **4.** b

Finding Information
1. Vicente Cabrera is a farmer.   **2.** His farm is in Mexico.
3. There is a hole in the fence.   **4.** Tomas went to the United States.   **5.** A U.S. Border Patrol officer found Tomas under a bush.   **6.** Tomas was alive.   **7.** Tomas was 15 miles from his home.

Understanding Pronouns
1. c   **2.** f   **3.** e   **4.** b   **5.** a   **6.** d

Making Inferences
1. T He works in the fields every day.   **2.** T Mr. Cabrera looked everywhere.   **3.** F "We need your help", they said.
4. T He was 15 miles from his home.

UNIT 8

Vocabulary
1. b   **2.** a   **3.** c   **4.** b

Understanding Details
1. chairs/sandwiches   **2.** small/big   **3.** money/weight
4. continue/stop   **5.** shoes/pants

Understanding Cause and Effect
1. c   **2.** d   **3.** a   **4.** b   **5.** e

Reviewing the Story
1. weighed   **2.** seat   **3.** back   **4.** die   **5.** diet   **6.** weight
7. woman   **8.** stop   **9.** pounds   **10.** married

UNIT 9

Vocabulary
1. One coin was missing.   **2.** She didn't count them.
3. She looked like picture 1.   **4.** A penny is a coin.

Understanding the Main Idea
1. a   **2.** c

Understanding Details
1. salad/cake   **2.** spoons/coins   **3.** angry/sick
4. supermarket/hospital   **5.** teachers/doctors
6. arm/throat   **7.** walking/talking

Understanding Pronouns
1. Marie   **2.** Marie   **3.** doctors   **4.** Marie   **5.** something small and black   **6.** the doctor   **7.** Marie

UNIT 10

Vocabulary
1. Max's parents buried him in the town cemetery.
2. She screamed and woke up.   **3.** She took his coffin out of the ground.   **4.** They went fast.

Understanding Details
1. lake/town   **2.** bathtub/bed   **3.** library/cemetery
4. wonderful/terrible   **5.** laughed/screamed
6. closed/opened   **7.** teacher/doctor   **8.** books/eyes

Understanding Pronouns
1. Max Hoffman   **2.** Max Hoffman   **3.** Max's mother
4. Max's mother   **5.** Max's mother   **6.** Max's parents and neighbor   **7.** Max's coffin   **8.** Max

Making Inferences
1. F In 1865, in a small town in Germany, a little boy was very sick.   **2.** F Max's mother had a terrible dream. She screamed in her sleep.   **3.** T But he wasn't lying on his back.   **4.** T A week later he was playing with his friends.   **5.** T He was 93 years old.

UNIT 11

Vocabulary
1. A cashier takes money at a store.   **2.** Children play with toys.   **3.** In a store people pay at the counter.   **4.** His ticket is a winning ticket.

Understanding Details
1. manager/cashier   **2.** parking/lottery   **3.** floor/counter
4. purse/tickets   **5.** $5/$50,000   **6.** ran/walked
7. uncle/mother   **8.** friendly/honest

Understanding Cause and Effect
1. c   **2.** d   **3.** a   **4.** b

Understanding Pronouns
1. Therese Costabile   **2.** people   **3.** Ms. Costabile
4. the tickets   **5.** the woman   **6.** the winning ticket
7. the woman   **8.** Ms. Costabile   **9.** her mother
10. her mother   **11.** Ms. Costabile

UNIT 12

Vocabulary
1. a 2. b 3. a 4. a 5. b 6. a

Finding Information
1. The Ten Bruins own a hotel. 2. A room with a TV is $14 a night. 3. The guests are noisy. 4. The guests are impolite.
5. The guests are pets.

Understanding Details
1. apartment/hotel 2. sandwich/carpet 3. loud/soft
4. workers/guests 5. children/pets 6. telephone/room
7. chocolate/medicine 8. tigers/cats

Understanding Pronouns
1. the hotel 2. the guests 3. people 4. people

UNIT 13

Vocabulary
1. a 2. a 3. b 4. a

Understanding the Main Idea
1. b 2. a

Finding Information
1. Jeff Keith ran across the United States. 2. He ran 3,200 miles. 3. He wore out 36 pairs of running shoes.
4. He talked to people about cancer. 5. People gave Jeff money. 6. The money is for the American Cancer Society.
7. Jeff ran for everybody.

Reviewing the Story
1. leg 2. artificial 3. run 4. wore 5. out 6. money
7. cancer 8. disabled 9. everybody

UNIT 14

Vocabulary
1. a 2. b 3. a 4. b

Understanding Details
1. umbrella/purse 2. slowly/fast 3. sleeping/walking
4. visited/chased 5. arms/ankles 6. school/jail
7. short/long

Understanding Pronouns
1. d 2. e 3. c 4. b 5. a

Making Inferences
1. F She had ten dollars in her purse. 2. F The thief was a young man. 3. F The thief will stay in jail for a long time.
4. F He had two broken ankles. The police took him to jail.

UNIT 15

Vocabulary
1. a 2. a 3. a 4. a

Understanding Details
1. sewing/sports 2. museum/gym 3. feet/muscles
4. secretary/body-builder 5. letters/awards
6. food/health 7. hungry/strong

Understanding Pronouns
1. b 2. a 3. e 4. d 5. c

Making Inferences
1. F I don't eat a lot of sweets. 2. T I eat a lot of fruit.
3. F I get plenty of sleep. 4. F I get plenty of fresh air.
5. F Body-building keeps me healthy.

UNIT 16

Vocabulary
1. b 2. b 3. b 4. a

Understanding Details
1. Onion/Union 2. uncle/father 3. days/months
4. washed/packed 5. with/without 6. carpenter/lawyer

Understanding Pronouns
1. e 2. b 3. d 4. a 5. c

Understanding Cause and Effect
1. b 2. d 3. a 4. c

UNIT 17

Vocabulary
1. a 2. b 3. b 4. b

Understanding Details
1. poor/rich 2. candy/money 3. states/newspapers
4. year/week 5. healthy/sick 6. mechanic/businessman
7. younger/older 8. cries/dies

Understanding Pronouns
1. d 2. c 3. e 4. b 5. a

Making Inferences
1. F Mr. Ross is a rich man. 2. F It is in 200 newspapers. Every week about 7,000 people write letters to Mr. Ross.
3. T Every week about 7,000 people write letters to Mr. Ross.
4. F Sometimes Mr. Ross doesn't send people money.
5. F When Mr. Ross was a boy, he was very poor.

Discussion
1. Yes 2. No 3. Yes 4. No
5. No (Mr. Ross sent her a cookbook.)

UNIT 18

Vocabulary
1. b 2. a 3. a 4. a 5. b

Understanding Details
1. brothers/sisters 2. years/months 3. sit/chew
4. chairs/wood 5. arms/cribs 6. suitcases/dresser
7. sold/ate 8. vegetables/dirt

Understanding Pronouns
1. b   2. c   3. f   4. e   5. d   6. a

Reviewing the Story
1. furniture   2. worried   3. chew   4. swallowed
5. cribs   6. handles   7. chair   8. dirt   9. wood
10. minerals   11. medicine   12. wood

UNIT 19

Vocabulary
1. a   2. a   3. b   4. a

Finding Information
1. It was a cold day in January.   2. Jimmy and his father were playing on a Chicago beach.   3. Jimmy ran onto the ice.
4. Jimmy fell into the cold water.   5. Firefighters pulled Jimmy out of the water.   6. Jimmy was in the water for over 20 minutes.

Understanding Details
1. mountain/lake   2. warm/cold   3. sand/snow
4. sled/ice   5. snow/water   6. church/hospital
7. talk/sleep   8. sick/healthy

Understanding Cause and Effect
1. d   2. e   3. b   4. a   5. c

Writing
    Jimmy was playing in the snow on a Chicago beach. His sled went onto the ice of Lake Michigan. Jimmy chased it. The ice broke, and Jimmy fell into the cold water.
    Twenty minutes later men pulled Jimmy out of the water. He was not breathing, and his heart was not beating. Paramedics worked on Jimmy for one hour. He began to breathe and his heart began to beat. Jimmy was alive. The paramedics rushed Jimmy to the hospital.
    After 13 weeks in the hospital Jimmy was healthy again. He was a strong little boy.

UNIT 20

Vocabulary
1. She is pouring milk.   2. They are the oldest children.
3. They brought these children into their home.   4. They make breakfast, lunch, and dinner.   5. Mr. and Mrs. Nason can do something special.

Understanding the Main Idea
1. a   2. b

Making Inferences
1. F He is frying 45 eggs.   2. F Some of the children are grown.   3. F They do not want to adopt older children.
4. T Mrs. Nason washes 12 loads of laundry every day.
5. T They are busy from five o'clock in the morning to 11 o'clock at night.

Reviewing the Story
1. children   2. adopted   3. babies   4. problems
5. home   6. home   7. work   8. laundry   9. cook
10. busy   11. ability   12. care

UNIT 21

Vocabulary
1. a   2. a   3. a

Understanding Details
1. airplane/ship   2. air/ocean   3. days/years   4. hungry/thirsty   5. drank/opened   6. bottle/dollar   7. telephoned/wrote   8. visit/help   9. scream/cry   10. sadness/happiness

Understanding Pronouns
1. the bottle   2. Hoa Van Nguyen   3. Hoa Van Nguyen
4. Hoa   5. Hoa   6. the bottle   7. his English
8. Mrs. Peckham   9. another letter   10. me and my family
11. the Nguyens and the Peckhams

Making Inferences
1. F Hoa used the dollar.   2. T Hoa got married at the camp.
3. F Hoa Van Nguyen, his wife, their baby, and Hoa's brother arrived at Los Angeles International Airport.   4. T Dottie and John Peckham were at the airport. Their tears were tears of happiness.

UNIT 22

Vocabulary
1. They traded food for the eggs.   2. There was no more fighting.   3. He couldn't stay.   4. The government said, "Yes, you can stay".

Understanding Details
1. French/Chinese   2. dentists/soldiers   3. I/II
4. beer/eggs   5. Spanish/English   6. days/years
7. England/the United States   8. student/visitor's

Understanding Cause and Effect
1. b   2. a   3. d   4. c

Reviewing the Story
1. food   2. traded   3. Two   4. Shoes   5. soldiers
6. dead   7. letter   8. visa   9. expired   10. let

ACKNOWLEDGMENTS

I wish to thank:

■my editor, Penny Laporte, for her meticulous editing and her long-distance encouragement;

■my colleague Sharron Bassano, for her creative suggestions for exercises;

■my colleague Peggy Miles, for her careful proofreading and her pragmatic solutions to the special problems writing a beginning reader poses;

■my principal, Orville Lindquist, for the graciously granted leave of absence;

■Clinton, Iowa residents Robert Seger, Edward Ridyard, and William Rolston, for their help in verifying the Max Hoffman story;

■the protagonists in the stories—Fast Eddy, Morgan Fairchild, Marion and David Ten Bruin, Louise Burt, Diana Vasquez, Percy Ross, Sandra Griffiths, Diane Nason, and Dorothy Peckham—for the details that added so much to the stories.